Food for the Seasons

By Professor Lun Wong and Kath Knapsey

Food for the Seasons

By Professor Lun Wong and Kath Knapsey

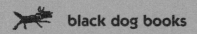 black dog books

First published in 2002 by

black dog books

15 Gertrude Street
Fitzroy Vic 3065
Australia
61 + 3 + 9419 9406
61 + 3 + 9419 1214 (fax)
dog@bdb.com.au
www.bdb.com.au

First published 2002
Reprinted in 2004

Design by Andrew Cunningham
Printed by Thomson Press (India) Limited

The National Library of Australia Cataloguing-in-Publication data:
Wong, Lun.

Food for the seasons.

Bibliography.
Includes index.
ISBN 1 876372 11 7.

1. Nutrition - Therapeutic use. 2. Eating (Philosophy).
3. Medicine, Chinese. I. Knapsey, Kath. II. Title

641.013

DISCLAIMER

In no way is this book a substitute for advice from a qualified medical practitioner.
If you are sick, seek professional help. While particular foods may be beneficial for
certain ailments, no one food should be eaten to excess – it is always important to
maintain a healthy variety in your diet.

ABOUT THE AUTHORS

Professor Lun Wong has spent most of the last sixty years steeped in traditional Chinese medicine. He has studied and travelled throughout China, India, Tibet and South-East Asia, gathering new insights, exchanging views with other practitioners, teaching and healing. Since 1974, Professor Wong has headed the Academy of Traditional Chinese Medicine Australia in Melbourne. The Academy provides an opportunity for people who wish to learn and practise traditional Chinese medicine, and it is also a source of succour for people who are sick. Professor Wong has lectured around the world on both traditional Chinese medicine and martial arts and has had several books published in Chinese. This is his first in English.

Kath Knapsey is a Melbourne-based writer with a long-standing interest in traditional Chinese medicine and an obsession with good food.

ACKNOWLEDGEMENT

Much appreciation is owing to Glenys Savage for her guidance, gentle comments, expertise in traditional Chinese medicine, organisational powers, attention to detail, drive and patience.

Contents

Introduction

How are you feeling? Do you have plenty of energy? Are you comfortable? Content? Do you look well? What you eat can make a difference. By listening to the needs of your body, you can change your responses to these questions for the better.

Sometimes it's hard to know if there's anything wrong with your body, or if you're just tired or worried about the kids or work. Sleep is the best cure for exhaustion, but if you get enough sleep and you're still always tired, a change in diet can help re-energise heavy muscles or a foggy head and help you see things in a different light.

There is a growing interest in what we are eating; an awareness that food can do more than fill an empty tummy. It's something the Chinese have known for thousands of years. Around 5000 BCE (Before the Common Era), the original texts on Chinese medicine were lost, but the teachings survived because they were handed down through families and by practitioners of traditional Chinese medicine (TCM). The *Huang Di Nei Jing* or *The Yellow Emperor's Classic of Internal Medicine* is one of the earliest surviving texts on TCM and was written more than three millennia ago. It is presented as a dialogue between the Yellow Emperor and his chief

Eat in moderation. Eat food prepared appropriately for the self and the season and enjoy a long and healthy life. – Confucius

•

TCM is life medicine because it encompasses prevention and healing, mind, body and spirit. – Professor Lun Wong

physician, Qi Bo. Within the pages of the *Huang Di Nei Jing*, reference is often made to the 'ancient people's way of life', so the understanding and practical advice it imparts is based on centuries of study that was already ancient by the time the *Huang Di Nei Jing* was written. For us today, TCM and the *Huang Di Nei Jing* offer an invaluable resource: a solid understanding of food therapy which uses an awareness of how different foods affect the way our organs interact with our internal energy flows, our minds and emotions.

For as long as I can remember, I've been interested in the body; trying to understand it and to understand how the external reacts to the internal. I don't mean just the physical, but everything that makes us who we are. And actually, what we can see, both physically and via behaviour, does offer clues about what is happening on the inside. What I've seen again and again over a lifetime of studying and treating clients, is that by using what we have, such as food and exercise, we can have a big impact on every aspect of our wellbeing. While having the clinic has, over the years, helped many thousands of people who have been sick, I also want to help people who are basically healthy to make the most of their good fortune. Before healing becomes necessary, there is an opportunity for prevention.

Food is a very important aspect of Chinese culture and everyday life for nearly every Chinese family. Within each family, special recipes and food traditions are passed down through the generations. Growing up, I took a great interest in food, not just for taste, but health too. I was aware that some foods were good for a cold and others helped ease a headache. Yet that wasn't so special; Chinese families took that knowledge for granted.

When Japan invaded Manchuria, I joined the Chinese army. I was very young – eighteen, I think. And I stayed in the army for the next 15 years, eventually becoming a colonel. But instead of forgetting my early fascinations with food and health, I spent all my holidays, evenings and spare time studying TCM. After the Sino-Japanese War, I got out of the army and spent the next five years travelling all around China studying different forms of TCM and also martial arts. I still have a real love for martial arts. To be able to properly practise physical arts, you need to understand each part of the body, how to use each part, and how to co-ordinate all the parts to act in unison. Doing so, directly strengthens the body for the prevention of ill-health. From another direction, this is the same understanding we need to make of food therapy too.

In 1949, I moved to Hong Kong. By this time, I was bursting with enthusiasm and all the understanding I had developed over the previous twenty years. I realised many people wanted to learn about TCM and martial arts, so I began to teach. When I moved to Australia in 1974, I set up the Academy of Traditional Chinese Medicine Australia so that I could bring what I know to more people.

Since coming to Australia, I have been back to China and travelled in other parts of Asia many times. It's been important and helpful to develop ties with TCM practitioners, training academies and universities of TCM so that we can share information and views on treatments and academic issues and gain new understanding from the old teachings. We have had a sister college near the Yellow River since 1987. The relationship with the Gansu College of Traditional Chinese Medicine in Lanzhou in Gansu Province, north-west China, has been very fruitful with many exchanges.

During the time I was travelling around China after the war, I went to Gansu Province to study the Fu Shi culture, which was being explored via several archaeology sites, to get a better understanding of Chinese history. The Fu Shi culture was where the I Ching, the book of change, came from. This culture existed around 8,000–10,000 BCE and it was obvious they were already using herbs as medicine. It was an exciting realisation.

Gansu Province is where the oldest teachings and practices come from; a logical place for learning and cultivation of knowledge because it was located along the Silk Road. Over the centuries, trade and the flow of travellers constantly brought new information and understanding of the world, philosophy and nature, including medicine and the human body. This constant exchange influenced many leaps in understanding. It also explains the close ties between Chinese, Tibetan and Indian (aryuvedic) medicines and why acupuncture has been practised in France for more than a thousand years and why the Greeks and Russians used suctioning cups on the back under similar principles as TCM.

As well as the recreated texts and the teachings passed down from master to student over the millennia, there have been unexpected discoveries. At a site in Gansu Province, a series of hundreds of caves house an incredible array of statues, paintings and images that portray culture and religion from between 1500 and 2000 years ago. When it was still common for Chinese to smoke tobacco in pipes up to a metre long, a smoker removed the ash from his pipe by tapping it on a wall in one of the caves. The sound was hollow. The false wall protected hundreds of old books, many of them about or with reference to traditional medicine.

Even older than the Fu Shi is Daoism. Although today, many people see Dao as a religion, originally it was purely the study of nature. Everything in nature is connected and in a continuous state of change. We are part of the patterns we can see around us. We have to develop an understanding of and cooperation with nature, just like the ants who know to move to higher ground when it's going to rain.

Like Dao, TCM theory acknowledges cycles in our lives. The seasons, and the weather changes they bring, affect our social behaviour, the sport we play, the way we dress, when bark falls off native gums and when leaves fall off deciduous trees. Wind, damp, heat, cold and dry are climatic conditions that accompany the seasons during the year. They affect our bodies from the outside and, from a TCM standpoint, they can also exist inside our bodies. And in just the same way that we react to the weather by trying to dress to keep cool in summer and warm in winter, we can eat foods that keep us internally warm in winter and cool in summer. By responding to our environment, we can avoid its extremes and maintain our own internal balance.

What may be surprising for us, but was instinctual knowledge for our ancestors, is that the fruit, vegetables and other foods that are available during each season are the very foods that contain exactly what we need to promote and maintain our health during that season. In losing our connection with the source of our foods, we have lost some of our intuitive awareness of foods. While all natural foods are good, each food has a specific time and way in which it should be eaten for us to get exactly what we need. Food plays such a ubiquitous role in our day, we forget it is a natural medicine to promote health and wellbeing. By explaining the principles of diet that have been developed over thousands of years, I can do for readers what I always try to do for the many clients who come to the clinic each year – help them to feel well as simply and as quickly as possible. Of course, particular conditions require individualised advice and treatments.

When I first started practising in Australia, some people thought Chinese medicine only suited people with a Chinese heritage; but what food is best depends on the place, the person and the season. The seasons occur at different times, and many of the foods are different, but the principles are the same. One thing to consider about China is that it is an enormous country encompassing wide diversities. China's people come from five different races, live in different climates and have inherited different eating habits. It would be impossible to stereotype the diets and

Tibetan and Chinese traditional medicines share a lot. The Tibetan Medical Thangka gives much advice, including what to eat: weak fellows should take meat and beer; in winter, take meat soup; during spring, take old highland barley; during summer, eat beef which is sweet; in autumn, take sweet, bitter and puckery foods. It also addresses the causes of disease – excessive contemplation, anger, envy, ignorance and work; and gives sage advice about how to live well – keep away from places where killing occurs and don't ride an untamed horse.

health of all Chinese people. Those in the south-east tend to eat more fish and more rice; in West China, people eat spicier foods; in the north, wheat is the staple grain; while those near the Mongolian border rely heavily on meat. Yet the principles of TCM work for them all, because TCM looks at each person as an individual and helps them work with their own bodies within the environment in which they live.

Many of the ingredients and recipes you'll find in Food for the Seasons wouldn't be found in a traditional Chinese cookbook. That's because you can use the principles of TCM without needing to limit your diet to one particular culture. One of the most important rules of TCM food therapy is to enjoy your meals and accept that food can make you feel great.

In Australia, even if we eat according to the seasons, everybody's dietary needs will differ. To work out what food is best for you at a given time, you need to consider several factors. What have you inherited in terms of diet and physiology? What is your age, gender, personality type, emotional state, activity level and body type? How is your health? These all play a role in determining whether you feel full of beans and ready to take on the world. Or not.

You can use food just to stop the hunger pains and to enjoy the taste in your mouth, or you can also use it to improve your health. Of course, for specific health concerns, it is always best to seek advice from a professional health practitioner but with the help of this book, food can become a medicine you use every day. So before you eat, think about how you feel and how you want to feel, and let tuning into the seasons become your way of life.

CHAPTER ONE

The basic principles of health

Treasures and pillars

Within TCM, there is a strong connection between body, mind and spirit. Everyone possesses three treasures: essence or life force, which is called jing; vital energy, which is qi (pronounced chee); and spirit and mind, known as shen. To live a healthy, long life, we need to cultivate jing, conserve qi and care for shen.

The treasures are supported by the four pillars: exercise, diet, rest and relaxation, and a good mental state. In this book, the focus is on diet because it's a good place to start – a tangible gateway into a new system of looking at health.

Yin and yang

Yin and yang are the two opposite and inter-dependent forms of energy inside our bodies. The idea of yin and yang is of oppo-site forces countering each other to create a balanced whole. In general terms, yin is cool and cold, deep, restful, lower, front and nourishing.

For the Greek philosopher, Epicurus (342–270 BCE) the goal of living was 'the health of the body and the freedom of the soul from disturbance'. This is almost identical to the Chinese view but for different reasons: the Chinese aim for longevity and Epicurus, for pleasure.

•

The principle of the interaction of the four seasons and of yin and yang is the foundation of everything in creation. Thus, sages nurture their yang in the spring and summer and their yin in the autumn and winter in order to follow the rule of rules: unified with everything in creation they maintain themselves continuously at the Gate of Life. – *Nei Jing*

Yang is the opposite force and is hot and warm, superficial, action, upper, back and eliminating. In medicinal and dietary terms, yin is substance and yang is function. Without substance there is no function and without function there is no reason for substance, so they are intertwined and each defines the other. For us, our physical bodies are the substance and our actions are the function. We gather new substance by function – we breathe, eat and drink. Without function, we could not take in the nutrients to support substance.

At different times of our lives, the energies of yin and yang interact differently. Children generate more substance than they consume, and therefore they grow. As we get older, our organs become less efficient and we do not produce enough substance to repair ourselves, and so our reserves of yin are run down. When all yin is gone, yang collapses and we die – and vice versa.

Yin – cold, deep, rest, lower, front, nourishing, chronic, deficiency, blood, female

Yang – hot, superficial, activity, upper, back, eliminating, acute, excess, energy, male

It is important to understand that yin and yang are only yin or yang in relation to each other. Nothing is purely yin or purely yang. Just as in the yin–yang symbol, each comes from the other and includes part of the other. For example, the lungs are usually considered to be yin, but they are located in the upper part of the body, which is considered yang, and the front of the body, which is considered yin. And the lungs contain both yin and yang qi within them. In the same way, many foods have both yin and yang qualities and effects. Heat is considered yang, but descending energy is thought to be yin, so if a particular food has these two characteristics, it becomes more complicated to label it a yin or yang food. But it does have yin and yang attributes and will be useful in your diet, depending on the effect you need.

Internally, if our yin quality is weak, we may experience feelings of uneasiness and anxiety – as if we are lacking some foundation or support. Yin affects bones, muscles, blood and fluids. It is what holds us up. Too much yin, which is cool, will overwhelm the heat and energy of yang. Most imbalances of yin are deficiencies, whereas most yang problems tend to be excesses. When yang is excessive, it tends to dry the yin fluids. Too much yang can block the body's energy paths and create heat that can show up as anger or impatience, which can destroy any sense of calm or wellbeing. Over time, a problem in either yin or yang will create an imbalance in the other.

Qi levels dictate the vitality of a person – what they do and how their body functions at every level. We get qi from the air we breathe, the food and drink we consume and what is stored in the kidneys as essence – which is made up of essence we inherit from our parents and excess qi from food and drink we have gathered in the past.

An example of yin and yang's close relationship is the interconnectedness between the qi and the blood. Qi, the body's energy flow, is yang and balanced by its yin counterpart, blood. Blood provides the nutrients to support qi and is considered the mother of qi. However, the relationship is reciprocal as qi leads and directs blood as it circulates in the body. Without strong qi, blood cannot be formed or circulate.

The quality of your blood can be seen in your appearance via your hair and skin tone. The effects and quality of your qi manifest more in movement. Harmonious qi produces graceful movement, abundant qi produces strength and insufficient qi manifests as weakness and clumsiness.

As in the yin–yang dichotomy, the aim of balance exists at every level of our lives. We aim to balance what happens inside our body with what is happening outside our body (in our environment) and for balance between the organs within the body. Since our bodies are living organisms, they are in a state of continuous change so balance is not a static goal – we have to keep working at it.

Digestion

To understand why it is helpful to eat in a certain way, it is important to consider what happens to food once it is inside us. Good digestion occurs when the body can extract the pure substances of food and can also expel as waste any elements that are not useful. Here, the stomach and the spleen are the most important organs. They are a zang–fu (yin–yang) pair. The spleen is zang (yin), which means it is the main or controlling organ in the pair and has several functions, while the stomach is the fu (yang) organ, which deals predominantly with the transportation of food.

After we've eaten, the spleen directs the digestion process and heats the stomach, which uses moisture (gastric juices) to break food down. The spleen uses its energy or qi to separate the purest parts of the food we eat. It drives pure food essence upwards to the lungs and assists in nourishing the heart and the blood and in aiding circulation. Within the lungs, pure food essence forms the basis for the creation of two types of qi: qi to support the body; and wei qi, the protective qi or immune system that stops disease getting in from outside the body. Wei qi is controlled by the lungs. Qi is controlled by the spleen. So, the spleen has an important role, creating qi, blood and immunity.

The stomach moves the rest of the meal to the large intestine to be expelled as waste. While the stomach depends on fluid for the digestion process and reacts adversely to dryness, the spleen reacts adversely to dampness. In the case of the spleen, too much water or dampness around this part of the body weakens the spleen's ability to promote digestion and

The beginning and root of all good is the pleasure of the stomach. – Epicurus

•

If you aren't getting enough nutrition, wei qi or immunity will be weak and you are likely to get sick.

•

According to the ancient philosopher Epicurus, a simple diet helps us appreciate the occasional luxury properly.

•

According to Confucius, the body, including the skin and hair, is a gift from our parents – therefore we shouldn't destroy it. To some, this goes as far as never cutting the hair.

•

Spleen qi pushes nutrition up and stomach qi pushes waste down. Poor posture after eating blocks the downward momentum of the stomach qi and impedes the ability of the spleen qi to move the nutrients up. If food is stuck in the stomach, it creates flatulence; if it is stuck too long, acids start to rise and the nutrient value of the food is destroyed. Take a stroll after eating.

extract the life supporting nutrients from the food. A weak spleen can mean malabsorption and eventual malnutrition, even in someone who has what appears to be a healthy diet. Often, in clinic, we see young women who eat what appear to be healthy meals, but they are struggling to find enough energy to drag themselves out of bed. This lack of energy is often based on a lack of nutrition because the spleen qi is very weak.

For optimal digestion, the temperature in the stomach should be slightly higher than in the rest of the body. If food is cold or raw, the stomach and spleen need to heat their contents before digestion can start. This heating takes more energy than if the food was hot or cooked. So, effective digestion is based on the ability of the spleen to change the form of pure food and drink essence, and push it up, and of the stomach to transport the rest of the food and drink down to the next stage in the process.

How much you eat is crucial. Under-eating will mean a lack of energy because there aren't enough nutrients consumed to support the qi. Going without food for half a day will cause a fall in the qi. Going without food for an entire day will exhaust the qi. At the other extreme, overeating squashes too much into the digestion system so that it can't work efficiently, so undigested food is left floating in the blood stream. This hurts both digestion and circulation. In other words, overloading the stomach blocks the qi. Especially important for older people is an understanding that overeating is bad for the heart. Manifestations of overeating are frequent or irregular bowel movements, frequent urination, disturbed sleep, poor digestion and an overweight body that makes exercise difficult.

Organ interconnectedness

Our internal organs and tissues all balance each other and work together in the same way the stomach and spleen do. Our major organs are called zang organs. These are yin and include the heart, lungs, spleen, liver and kidneys. These organs generate and store essence. The fu organs are yang and their main function is to receive and transport what we eat and drink. These include the stomach, small intestine, large intestine, gallbladder and bladder. Each zang organ has a fu partner.

> **Each zang organ has a fu partner**
>
> heart – small intestine
> lungs – large intestine
> spleen – stomach
> liver – gallbladder
> kidneys – bladder

These pairs work together and the health and strength of each affects the other. So if the spleen is strong, it will strengthen the stomach, whereas if the spleen is weak, it will not support the stomach sufficiently and eventually the weakness of the spleen will spread to the stomach.

As well as affecting a fu organ, each zang organ is interacting and inter-promoting with the other zang organs. Look at the 'Organs support and control cycle diagram' (page 8). Within the support cycle, which can be seen as a mother–child relationship, the spleen supports the lungs, the lungs support the kidneys, the kidneys support the liver, the liver supports the heart and the heart supports the spleen. While the mother is strong, it can feed the child; but if the mother becomes weak, it won't be able to feed the child properly. On the other hand, if the child becomes excessive and greedy, it steals energy from the mother and causes the mother to become weak. For example, the kidneys support the liver by providing yin fluids. If the kidneys fail to provide enough fluid, the liver will overheat. This can cause insomnia, aggressive behaviour or feelings of frustration. If the liver becomes excessive, it will steal too much fluid from the kidneys, putting them out of balance with possible consequences including ringing in the ears and aching knees.

Organs support and control cycle

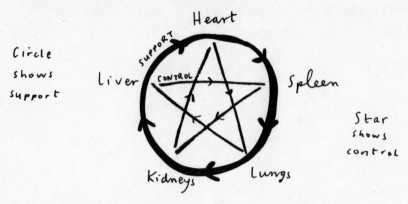

The other major relationship between the zang organs is known as the husband and wife relationship or the control cycle. If an organ becomes unbalanced it can reverse the control cycle and attack the organ it is supposed to contain. The most common example of this is an excessive liver that attacks the spleen – anger (which is the emotion connected to the liver) hurts digestion and the ability to absorb nutrients from food. So to protect the spleen, one option is to strengthen the lungs because the liver is usually kept in check by the lungs. It is a delicate balance. Every organ must be strong in order for the body to be truly balanced and healthy.

Each organ has its own qi, which has a certain pattern it should flow in. While the organs are healthy and the energy channels open, qi flows in the appropriate directions. The heart qi follows the blood vessels everywhere they go around the body to the tips of the limbs. The spleen qi moves up. The stomach qi moves down. The lung qi moves down and spreads everywhere. The kidney yin qi moves upward to balance the heart. The kidney yang qi moves up to pull the lung qi down to every part of the body so that all our cells receive oxygen. And the strong downward pressure of the lung qi on the large intestine ensures easy bowel movements. Liver qi is floating and happy, as long as it isn't blocked. When we experience anger, liver qi is rocking the body instead of floating. Vomiting is stomach qi flowing in reverse.

The organs also interact with other tissues in the body. The face can be seen as the mirror of the heart. The heart governs vessels, opens to the tongue and is enriched by the blood. The lungs are reflected by the skin and open to the nose. The spleen reflects externally on the lips and flesh. It also affects the muscles and opens to the mouth. The liver is reflected in the nails. It also affects the tendons and opens to the eye. The kidneys are reflected in the hair, affect the bone marrow and open to the ear.

So, if your organs aren't working well, it will be obvious in your appearance via your hair, face, skin, eyes and nails. If your hair is dull and lifeless or greasy and lank, it might be more effective to eat foods to support your kidneys than to change shampoo. You can follow the links further. The lungs open to the nose and a runny nose is often the first sign of germs attacking the lungs. The lungs also affect voice and sense of smell.

The major organs have a strong impact on everything that makes us who we are. Spirit-mind or shen is stored in the heart; soul, in the lungs; mood, in the liver; idea, in the spleen; and willpower, in the kidney. Perhaps, on an instinctual level, there has long been an awareness of the influence of

The two major relationships between the zang organs are the mother–child relationship, in which the mother feeds and supports the child; and the husband and wife relationship, where exuberance of an organ is constrained by its spouse.

•

A holistic diagnosis considers not just the aching limb, but the entire body, mind and spirit of the client.

– Professor Lun Wong

•

The health of the heart shows in the face; the lungs, on the skin; the spleen, in the flesh and muscles; the liver, in the nails and eyes; and the kidneys, in the hair.

•

Aristotle sought balance for the emotions and wrote about the inappropriateness of both excess and deficiency. He said, 'To have courage is the middle ground or virtuous mean; rash confidence, the excess; and cowardice, the deficiency.'

> When someone is sick and becomes angry, impatient or upset, I listen to them, but I don't get angry in response. I want to help. If someone is unwell, to react to an outburst is to catch their sickness.
> – Professor Lun Wong

our organs as Shakespeare referred to someone in a bad mood as having a black liver and courage is often linked to the heart.

Emotions are closely linked to the organs. If our organs are healthy and balanced, we are far more likely to be in a balanced emotional state. Of course, this doesn't mean that if your organs are healthy, you won't feel emotional highs and lows. Rather your emotional responses will be in proportion to the stimulus they receive from the outside world. As an example, fear is based in the kidneys and if your emotions and organs are balanced, your reaction to a fearful situation should also be balanced. If you are attacked, you will feel enough fear to run or defend yourself, but not so much fear that you freeze and are not able to do anything to avoid the assault. Decision-making is based in the gallbladder. Anger comes from the liver and is useful to harness energy and get things done. If your liver is balanced, you won't fly into a rage simply because the driver on the road in front of you is going at ten kilometres below the speed limit.

The table below summarises how the organs are linked to each other, to the body and to emotions.

Organ interconnectedness					
Zang organ	liver	heart	spleen	lungs	kidneys
Fu organ	gallbladder	small intestine	stomach	large intestine	bladder
Sense organ	eyes	tongue	mouth	nose	ears
Effects	tendons	blood vessels	muscles	energy	bones
Reflection	nails	face	lips	skin	hair
Emotion	anger	joy	worry	grief	fear

CHAPTER TWO

Food and the elements of climate

Damp, heat, wind, cold and dry are the environmental elements that cycle with the seasons and create our weather. These same elements can exist within the body at any time of year, however, they are likely to be more extreme in the season they correspond to as the weather creates and promotes the conditions in which imbalances thrive. What happens inside our bodies is influenced by the weather and the effects of the seasons, and also by our food intake, genetic make-up, body type, and emotional and mental wellbeing. So to have a balanced diet, we need to consider our body and the effects of the environment.

Energies of food

Different foods have different natures or capacities to generate different temperatures within the body and these can affect our internal organs and their balance. The nature of food isn't necessarily connected to the temperature of the food at the time of consumption, and it is the food's nature that has a more lasting effect on our internal temperature. Warm and hot foods warm the body; cool and cold foods have the opposite effect. For instance, alcohol can be full of iceblocks, but still heats us internally.

Most people do best by consuming a predominantly gentle, warming diet. Cold and hot foods have important roles to fulfil within the body, but should be used in moderation. While many vegetables, grains and legumes are neutral, the cooking process tends to make them warming.

Here are some general guidelines on how to guess whether a food may be warming or cooling.

- Plants that take longer to grow, such as cabbage, parsnips and carrots, are often more warming. Lettuce and cucumbers are more cooling plants.
- Raw food is more cooling than the same food will be after cooking.
- Food eaten cold is more cooling.
- Foods cooked for a longer time tend to be more warming, as are foods cooked with oil.
- Chewing well means food in the stomach is more warming because it doesn't take as much internal energy to break down.
  This logic also applies to food finely chopped, mashed or pureed.

Like the natures of food, our bodies can be hot, warm, cool or cold. Or a mixture. People with a hot constitution should aim for balance by eating cool and warm foods, but avoiding hot foods. Although it might seem logical for a person with a hot body type to eat mainly cold foods, it is important not to injure the stomach and the spleen, which need to be warm to work effectively. Without good digestion, the entire body suffers. If you have a cold constitution, you should aim to warm your body by eating foods that are warm and hot, both in nature and temperature. If your system is naturally hot, alcohol will be more damaging for you than for someone with a cooler body.

It's best to avoid eating large amounts of foods that are in the extremes of hot and cold because, over time, these are likely to create imbalances that lower our defences against disease. Foods that affect our internal temperature on an extreme level often have only a short-term influence. Both alcohol and chillies heat the body quickly, but the effect fades almost as fast. Heat rises and cold sinks, so in some cases, eating something very hot will make the top of the body hotter without warming the lower body and will actually exacerbate imbalance rather than improving balance. If you are cold, it is better to eat warming foods rather than hot, so the effect will be more long-lasting.

In general, when treating chronic (long-term) or cold problems it is better to use a gentle, slow-working remedy. In TCM, this is referred to as protecting the righteous qi – fixing what's wrong without damaging what's right. Faster remedies are more appropriate for acute (short-term) or heat problems such as a head-cold with fever.

Flavours and directions of food

All foods have a flavour. The five flavours of food are sour, bitter, sweet, pungent and salty. Many foods are a combination of more than one flavour. Grapes are sweet and sour. Celery is sweet and bitter. Turnip is pungent and bitter. Kohlrabi is pungent, sweet and bitter.

Once in the body, each flavour enters a different organ (see 'The destination of the flavours', page 14). In small amounts, these flavours benefit and strengthen their corresponding organs. The sweet flavour affects the spleen and the flesh and comes from foods such as honey, rice, beef, cherries and peas. The salty flavour affects the kidneys and bones and comes from foods such as salt, seaweed and crab. The pungent flavour affects the lungs and energy and comes from foods such as onions, fennel, chives, cloves and coriander. The sour flavour affects the liver and tendons and comes from foods such as lemons, pears, plums and mangoes. The bitter flavour affects the heart and blood and comes from foods such as alfalfa, rye and lettuce.

The destination of the flavours
sweet to the spleen
salty to the kidneys
pungent to the lungs
sour to the liver
bitter to the heart

A balanced diet that takes all five flavours into account does not mean an equal percentage of each flavour. A balanced diet is a diet dominated by sweet foods and includes small amounts of each of the other flavours each day. Sweet refers to most grains, legumes, vegetables, nuts, seeds and fruit. This is just one more indication of how central the health of the digestive system is to our overall health.

An appropriate mix of the five tastes creates a diet that strengthens the bones, makes the tendons flexible, promotes the circulation of blood and qi, and keeps the skin and muscles in good condition. However, in excessive amounts, the flavours damage the organs they usually help. While sweet foods (in the form of vegetables, grains, legumes, fruit and meat) usually dominate the diet, there should still be a balance. Sweetness improves the appetite and strengthens digestion, but too much of the sweet flavour injures the muscles, harms digestion, can make the hair fall out because it hinders nutrient absorption and causes unhealthy weight gain. Since refined sugar is so prevalent in our diet, many people battle with the bulge.

The flavours each have a further effect on the body. Sweet foods boost the qi, engender fluids and can neutralise the toxic effects of other foods. Bitter foods are astringent and dry, reduce body heat and lead the qi downwards, but too much harms the heart and dries the skin. Sour foods astringe and constrain, which is very useful to check diarrhoea and excessive perspiration, whereas too much can cause cracked lips and overly tight tendons. Pungent foods promote energy circulation, lead the qi up and outwards and tend to be drying, although too many tend to weaken the body's qi. Salty foods lead the qi down and soften hardness, but too much of the salty flavour slows the flow of the blood and harms circulation. Moderation in all things is the key.

The nutrient essence of some foods moves outward towards the skin and body surface, of others, it moves inward to the centre of the body, others, up above the waist and others, below the waist. Depending on the season and the state of your health, these movements can make you more or less balanced. In general, what determines which way a food moves is the mix of its temperature and flavour. Hot and pungent foods move out, sweet and warm foods move up, cool and salty or sour foods move down and cold and bitter foods move in.

So why does direction matter? Because seasons, body types and ailments all have particular directions. In general, foods that move up or out can be used to support the up and outward seasons (spring and summer), to counteract downward ailments and to balance yin body types. Foods that move down or in are used to support the in and downward seasons

Pungent and sweet foods are yang and warming and they direct energy up and out. Bitter, sour and salty foods are yin and cooling and they direct energy down and in.

•

Foods marinated in rice wine will move upwards in the body; which may be helpful if you have a head-cold.

(autumn and winter), to counteract ailments that flow up and to balance yang body types. For example, hiccupping is considered an upward ailment and should be treated with a downward moving food such as an orange or tangerine. Certain ailments, such as a headache, stay in a specific area of your body. So, the food to ease a headache will need to have an upward motion so it reaches the pain area.

By knowing the direction a food moves and taking account of the season, we can work out which food in winter will help balance a thin woman with aches in her knees and lower back. Or in summer, which food for a red-faced, middle-aged man with high blood pressure. Or in spring, which food for an angry teenager with acne. Or ...

Upward-moving foods are helpful for diarrhoea and those that move down can ease vomiting, hiccupping and asthma. Notice how the direction of the symptom is treated with a food that moves in the opposite direction. Food can also be fast or slow moving. Glossy or sliding foods tend to move faster, while obstructive foods are slower. Glossy foods include honey and spinach and are good to treat constipation, while obstructive foods, such as olives, are useful to treat diarrhoea.

The way a particular food moves within the body can be changed by the method of cooking or by other foods with which it is mixed. For example, anything marinated in wine is likely to move upwards; foods cooked with vinegar tend to become obstructive; foods cooked with ginger juice move outward; while salt tends to draw food down. Generally, hot or warm foods with a pungent or sweet flavour move up or up and out, while cool and cold foods with a sour, salty or bitter flavour move in or in and down.

Eating with the seasons

There are two ways of eating according to the seasons. The first is to follow the patterns of a season, and the second is to use opposite influences to maintain a balance. By eating foods that move the energy down to the core of the body to regenerate and repair in winter, we take advantage of the strength of winter. In the warmer months of the year, we can eat foods that move the energy up to support increased activity and elimination (such as perspiration and regular bowel movements) so energy and blood circulate well. At the same time, it is important to find a balance in each season – as we do when we wear a coat to stay warm in the cold of winter.

The natural pattern in spring is sprouting and it is best to eat foods that move upwards during the months of spring. In summer, there is strong growth, so the most beneficial foods are those that move outward. Outward moving foods encourage perspiration which helps keep us cool in summer. Autumn is the time for harvesting many crops and foods that move down are most suitable. As winter is the time for storage, food that moves inward is appropriate then.

Each season has a corresponding organ that is more sensitive during this time. Each season is also balanced with an awareness of what came before it and what will come after.

A season for each organ
spring – liver
early summer – heart
late summer – spleen
autumn – lungs
winter – kidneys

If you eat inappropriately in one season, you will suffer in that season and you will also increase the health risk in the next season because you will be badly prepared. To get very obsessive with the direction of one season will make it more difficult to adapt to the next season. In winter, for example, we store heat to help counteract the cold weather, however, when spring comes with its rising qi, too much heat left over from winter can cause diarrhoea. Even within each season you can respond to specific weather patterns.

Wind – While it can occur in any season, spring is the season of wind as there is a sense of waking, sprouting and shifting after the winter. Internally or externally, wind can be wild and unpredictable, unsettling, hot or cold. Autumn has plenty of wind too, but the effect in autumn is more likely to be drying because of the heat and dryness of the summer that has just passed. Wind can enter the body via the skin or an orifice and interrupt the circulation of the qi. Once inside the body, internal wind shows up as jerky movements, lack of coordination, dizziness or disease that has symptoms that are unpredictable and come and go without sense or reason (such as hives). Wind in the environment can be responsible for the common cold and flu, aches and pains in joints and muscles and some headaches. Internal wind is often created by blockages and can cause vertigo, tremors, headaches, seizures, stroke and emotional instability. Wind also breaks down the body's defensive qi and lets in the other elements as well. Internal wind can be caused by imbalance in the liver and the channels the liver qi flows through. Excessive heat in the blood can generate wind too. Deficient blood creates empty spaces within the blood vessels and these spaces are taken up by internal wind.

Heat – Heat is most likely in summer, but can occur in the body during any season. It speeds metabolism, dilates blood vessels, activates circulation and moves up and out. Too much heat can cause red, swollen and painful inflammation, rapid pulse, fever, thirst, dryness, constipation, difficult urination and agitation. Heat moving to the surface causes perspiration and, as it reaches the surface, can induce acne, sores, ulcers, boils and rashes. Heat can come from the environment, exercise, adrenaline, disease, diet and excessive emotions.

Damp – Dampness occurs in the environment most often in late summer, but can occur in any season depending on the weather conditions. It is slow and heavy, sinking and hard to move. In nature it is humidity or a swamp. In the body, it is swelling and heaviness, a build-up of fluids and excess secretions that cause stagnation and obstruction of circulation. Dampness manifests in feelings of sluggishness, apathy and dullness. On the skin, it shows up as oiliness and sticky perspiration. Internally, it is phlegm, mucus, water retention around the stomach, dull pain, fluid build-up, swollen joints and lethargy. Damp often occurs together with cold, heat or wind. With damp cold, circulation is constricted, resulting in fatigue and stiff, sore muscles and joints. Damp heat may manifest as red, painful swellings, thick discharge, blisters, inflammations and sores with pus or fluid. Damp wind causes bubbly phlegm, itching sores and swelling that comes and goes.

Dry – Dryness inside the body is most intense in autumn. The wind in autumn makes it more difficult than usual to get enough air into the lungs. Like the leaves of deciduous trees that wither and shrivel, our lungs can get very dry when it's windy. Dryness can manifest as brittle nails and hair, cracked and wrinkled skin, dry nostrils, irritated eyes, constipation or dry stools, lack of perspiration and small amounts of urine. While dryness is most intense in autumn, internal dryness may occur at any time if the production and use of bodily fluids is harmed by heat, profuse perspiration, prolonged diarrhoea, excessive urination or loss of blood.

Cold – Cold is most prevalent in winter. Cold slows and depresses both metabolism and circulation. Cold from the environment causes skin and muscle contraction, shivering and goose bumps. Cold inside the body can come from the environment or from consuming cold food and drinks or it can be a result of yang deficiency. A long illness, poor diet or exposure to cold can weaken the yang and allow cold to dominate the body. This can be especially hard on the digestive system because the stomach and spleen need heat to transform and transport what we eat. Cold in the digestive system can cause a weak immune system that, in turn, can lead to asthma, colitis, arthritis and eczema.

Sometimes, conditions in the body aren't caused, but are exacerbated, by that condition in the environment. For example, dampness is most often caused by overeating or by eating too much sweet, greasy food. However, dampness in the body can be made much worse by a damp environment. Climatic conditions can cause sickness in the body that manifests as something else. Depending on the person, dryness in the body may be brought on by heat, dryness, wind or cold in the environment.

Food for all seasons

There are some foods that we can eat in all or any season but that doesn't mean we are ignoring seasonal influences. Tofu is an excellent example, as are grains, of food that can be adapted to suit both seasonal and individual requirements. In spring, to support growth, tofu can be included in meals such as thick soups, steamed fish or boiled with vegetables and beans and a little meat. In summer, tofu can be added to clear soup. In autumn, tofu should be fried lightly until the edges are crispy and then added to a vegetable stew. In winter, tofu should be fried thoroughly, then added to a dish including vegetables, oil and meat. Because we need to store up energy against the cold, winter dishes tend to be heartier and include more oil than meals in other seasons. Oil and meat also offset the cooling effect of the tofu which would otherwise be too cooling for winter.

CHAPTER THREE

Reading your body

The human yin–yang table

It's quite easy to get a general idea of whether you are a yin or yang type by looking at your general personality and how you relate to the world. Of course, people can be mixtures of yin and yang.

Yang	Yin
outgoing	introverted
aggressive	timid
quick	slow
red complexion	pale complexion
focused mind	serene
warm body	cool body
dry skin	moist skin
tense, strong body	limp, weak body
desire-filled	complacent
loud voice	soft voice

If you don't know where to start, look in the mirror and stick out your tongue – is it a healthy pink with a thin white coat?

•

A person with a thin, long, red tongue is always talking – never stops.
– Professor Lun Wong

•

The phlegm you cough up is telling – for a start, you have phlegm. White indicates cold; yellow indicates heat; green indicates wind. Bubbles in the phlegm indicate cold from the stomach.

•

Sometimes I have been surprised at the colour of a person's tongue – until I find out they've just eaten green lollies or liquorice.
– Professor Lun Wong

At different times in their lives, most people fall in between these extremes, at least in some of the listed areas. And there are subtleties to consider. For example, when yin is weak, yang may look strong but it's only a relative strength. So a person may have a loud voice and have plenty of wants, but still be fundamentally a yin type.

On a more specific level, the tongue acts as our personal health chart – once you get used to this idea, you'll find yourself sticking your tongue out in front of the mirror every time you feel a little off-centre. Most imbalances in the body show up on the tongue, and it is possible to do a basic diagnosis by yourself. For specific concerns, you should see a professional health practitioner. There are three things to look at when checking your tongue – substance, colour and coating.

In the same way that different parts of the tongue register different flavours, different imbalances in the body show themselves in different ways on the tongue. A healthy tongue fits neatly in the mouth, is smooth, moist, pink, firm and has a thin white coating on the surface.

A thin tongue shows there is weak heart qi. Teeth marks on the sides of the tongue also suggest a lack of qi in general. Swelling on the sides of the tongue indicates a liver imbalance. A fat tongue shows you are retaining a lot of fluids. Indents up the middle suggest the body is run down and may also indicate that you are not getting enough sleep or that you have yin deficiency or that you have a weak digestion system that is not accessing enough nutrients in your diet. Either way, it shows the body is run down and needs better care.

Diagram of a tongue

Labels on diagram: Kidneys, Spleen, Liver, Liver, Lungs, Lungs, Heart

Tongue colour should be similar to the inside of your bottom lip. Very red indicates heat, while very pale suggests cold with weakness. A yang deficiency shows up as a pale tongue and is usually accompanied by signs of cold. If the tongue is pale and very wet, it indicates damp in the body. A white coat indicates cold, a yellow coat indicates heat and a black coat shows extreme heat over a long period. A red tip suggests imbalance in the heart which can include stress, over-thinking about problems or not drinking enough liquids. Green is always related to the liver, and red on the sides shows heat in the liver. A thick and sticky coating indicates damp. The thicker the coating, the more long-term the condition.

With all this, there is an important thing to remember – be flexible. Even within the course of a common cold, your body may change from cold (clear, runny mucus) to hot (thick, yellow mucus). Just because a remedy is useful for you today, doesn't mean it will be appropriate tomorrow or that the same remedy will help your uncle next week.

Use the table, 'The seasons and the organs' (page 24), to help bring information on the seasons, organs and tastes together. Remember that balance is the most important point about TCM food therapy. Let's take spring, for example. Spring is the natural time to eat less and shrug off extra winter weight. Spicy foods actually increase appetite and may aggravate the liver so rather than relying on spicy foods to add taste, use sesame oil. Sour foods can draw down liver fire. As many people tend to have a strong liver, it is actually better to avoid the liver boost provided by fire foods during spring.

The seasons and the organs					
Season	Organ	Taste	Meat	Include	Limit
SPRING	liver	sour	goat	sesame	spicy
SUMMER	heart	bitter	lamb	wheat	salty
LATE SUMMER	spleen	sweet	beef	rice	sour
AUTUMN	lungs	pungent	chicken	spicy foods	bitter
WINTER	kidneys	salty	pork	beans/ lentils	sweet

For most people, becoming familiar with TCM principles doesn't mean having to give up their favourite foods. There's plenty of wisdom in many traditional cuisines. Consider pasta with pesto. Wheat is mixed with egg to make the pasta and pine nuts and basil are the main ingredients for the pesto. Wheat, eggs, and pine nuts are highly nutritious foods and, if digestion is sluggish, they can cause damp. But the basil in the pesto eliminates dampness. Wheat is cool, whereas pine nuts are warm and get rid of wind. So this is a good meal for most healthy people as it is balanced in several ways.

There are a few final basics to discuss before we get onto the seasons. Cooking times are an important part of good digestion. While it is fine to cook vegetables for short periods, especially in summer, grains, legumes and some vegetables such as sweet potato always need to be very well-cooked as, rather than providing extra nutrients, undercooking these foods hurts digestion. Legumes are a good example. Some people avoid legumes completely because legumes can cause flatulence, but actually, this problem may be fixed by increasing the cooking time and making a few other small changes. Here are a few ways to minimise the flatulence-producing effects of legumes.

Soak legumes overnight. Discard soak water and bring to the boil in fresh water. Reduce the heat and simmer covered until almost cooked (three hours for kidney beans and turtle beans, one and a half hours for adzuki beans, one hour for lentils, mung beans, black-eyed peas and split peas). Add spices and cook for a

further fifteen minutes. Make sure the legumes are soft. Remove the lid and allow excess water to steam off. If you are cooking lentils, add a tablespoon of apple cider vinegar for the final twenty minutes of cooking to make them easier to digest. Try adding fennel or cumin during the cooking process, but never salt, as salt toughens the outer layer and makes legumes even harder to digest. For more flavour and nutrients and for easier digestion, add a piece of soaked kombu or kelp to the pot before adding the legumes.

Garlic is another ingredient we need to consider. If you are living in a very cold, damp climate in the mountains, regularly eating garlic is helpful, but it is not so helpful if you are in the warmth of the city. Once garlic gets inside the body, it's quite bossy. It pushes out worms and toxins and can increase the energy which is good, but in excess, its strength can have a negative effect on qi, sending the qi in the wrong direction or strengthening an organ that is already too strong. This can actually make some common colds worse and it can cause skin outbreaks, poor digestion or feelings of anger and frustration. Raw garlic is spicy and too much can harm the liver. Garlic creates internal fire, especially in the liver, so if you tend to feel angry, impatient or aggressive, or if you have stomach fire, garlic may be too strong for you. One way to soften the effects of garlic is to eat it with vinegar, which is astringent and can limit garlic's exuberance. In northern China, where garlic is eaten copiously, it is usually eaten with vinegar.

Although it is becoming more popular, vegetarianism may not be the best choice for some people. People who traditionally flourish on a vegetarian diet tend to live a spartan life with a high level of spirituality and few physical demands or live in a warm or tropical climate. For people in a temperate climate, leading a busy, modern life with the pressures of work, family and money, vegetarianism may not supply all the necessary nutrients and dietary support required. Thin or weak people who rarely include meat in a meal can build up their strength with meat. If you can't face the idea of eating chunks of meat, a soup that uses meat stock or fish sauce can help. Meat that makes up twenty per cent of a meal, twice a week, is enough for most people. Usually, meat should be more like an extra bonus than the main focus of the meal. Too much meat makes strong people aggressive and unsatisfied with life and overwhelms the digestive system causing damp, heat and general excess.

●

Using what nature provided, the ancient herbalists and health practitioners of many cultures shared similar views on health and healing. It is hoped that as you read this book, you will find inspiration to enjoy the offerings of each season and discover small facts and ways of looking at food that make innate sense to you.

CHAPTER FOUR

Spring and its recipes

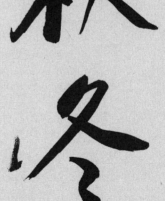

Spring is the time to get up and do. It is the season of activity. A time of stirring after the cold of winter. It is the season of wind, both in the environment and our bodies. Spring is the season to eat foods with upward energies, such as young, green, sprouting, above-ground vegetables.

With the onset of spring, we start to loosen up as energy in the body begins to move up. Spring is naturally the time to nurture yang, our action principle. Appetite eases as the body shakes off the need to store energy as it did over the colder months. With the environment's subtle support as the weather changes, people who want to lose weight can take advantage of the natural trends of spring to help them do more and eat less.

Wind

In Australia, wind is a potent force and can occur in any season, but appreciating its effect specifically in spring is important because spring is the time the liver is most sensitive – and the liver is very susceptible to the effects of wind. Wind appears quickly, can change without warning and is as destabilising as it is unpredictable. If you have internal wind – whether it comes from the environment or has been created inside your body (not flatulence – see page 18) – you may experience some of the following symptoms: dizziness, cramps, itching, spasms, tremors, pain that comes and goes, vertigo, twitching, pulsating headaches, ringing in the ears or dryness in the upper body. On an emotional level, wind can cause manic-depression, nervousness, inability to settle or make commitments, agitation, nervousness and emotional turmoil. Internally, wind often moves other conditions around such as heat or cold in the form of fever, moving pains or the common cold. Within the body, wind can be caused by excess heat, yin deficiency or stagnation of the liver.

There are several foods that naturally reduce the effects of wind. In early spring (and if you tend to be more yin), try oats, pine nuts, prawns, ginger, fennel and basil. Later in the season (or if you are more yang), choose celery, mulberry, strawberry and peppermint. Other foods that limit the effects of wind include black or yellow soybean (cooked until soft), black or yellow sesame seed, sage and chamomile. Foods such as crabmeat, eggs and buckwheat can aggravate wind symptoms.

The organs of spring

The liver and the gallbladder are the internal organs that are in the spotlight during spring. If the liver and gallbladder are supported and balanced during spring, the entire body will benefit immediately and be set up with the best possible health foundation to be strong and well in the seasons to come.

What you learn about the liver in this chapter, you can apply to benefit your liver all year, using the foods of each season. According to TCM, the main functions of the liver are to store blood, support the heart and to create and maintain a smooth and calm flow of qi throughout both the body and mind. When the liver is balanced and functioning well, liver qi is a happy, active, floating qi. It helps us get things done effectively without stress.

What we eat, and how we eat it, plays a part in how we feel and how we express our feelings. People with a healthy liver and gallbladder are calm, make decisions easily and are stress-free. The liver stores emotional issues we haven't dealt with, so it can be the home of anger and frustration. It is also the home of mood. When the liver is not functioning well, or the qi is trapped or forced up, we can experience physical and emotional consequences. Someone with a less than healthy liver may be operating on an emotional rollercoaster, feeling resentment, aggression, edginess and impulsive behaviour. In the longer term, these emotions can lead to depression.

From the outside, the health of the liver shows in our eyes, fingernails and toenails

Colds, flu and vertigo can often be linked to wind in the body. While it doesn't seem fair to get sick just as the cold weather seems to be easing, a windy spring can unbalance the body and allow flu to take hold.

•

Wind is often present with another element such as cold or heat. Wind heat can enter the body as a germ via the nose and throat.

•

If you wake up with a cold head in the mornings, your yang may need a boost. One of the easiest ways to strengthen yang is to top meals with finely chopped spring onions.

•

The liver can be an emotional minefield, or your best ally in getting the job done.

•

Rheumatoid arthritis affects the joints and osteoarthritis affects the bones. Many cases of arthritis can be linked to wind caused by liver stagnation. If pain moves around, it could be wind. Try eating celery, sage, oat porridge, fennel or coconut.

and can be felt in our tendons. Nails should be strong and unblemished with pink beds and white tips. If the storage facility of our liver is working well, the tendons will mirror that ability to respond, being strong, yet flexible. The same thing applies to anger – it can be a very useful emotion when related to determination (but not if it is excessive), and it should be let go of when we are done with it. To see the health of the liver on the tongue, check the sides. If the liver is in perfect shape, the tongue will be firm, pink and have a light, white coat. If the sides of your tongue are swollen, flabby or bruised-looking (or there is a greenish tinge anywhere on the tongue), then spring is the perfect time to start getting your liver in shape. This means the central part of spring dietary balance is supporting and calming the liver while also toning up the other organs so they can hold their own against bullying from the liver.

The sour flavour

Sour is connected to the liver. Sour strengthens the liver and is yin and cooling. It has a contracting, astringent effect and dries and firms. It helps strengthen tendons, improve bladder control and ease incontinence, excessive sweating, diarrhoea, sagging skin, haemorrhoids and prolapses. Once eaten, sour heads straight for the liver. A small amount of the sour flavour is essential for a balanced liver, but too much will make the liver too strong and cause imbalance between the organs. Overeating sour foods can damage the tendons by making them too tight. People with constipation should mainly avoid sour foods, as astringent foods can make constipation worse. Examples of sour foods include lemons, limes, hawthorn fruit, pickles and rosehip. Vinegar is also sour.

As you read about the liver, you'll realise that for many people, the liver is too strong in spring, so for the most part, these people should avoid sour-flavoured foods in spring. Pungent foods also affect the liver and clear wind from the body and, in moderation, will be the best accompaniment to the full sweet flavours of vegetables and grains.

Liver yin deficiency

People with general deficiency are weak, withdrawn, have a soft voice and shallow breath. It's important for people with a deficiency to eat gentle nutritious food – full sweet flavours such as legumes and vegetables rather than the less substantial sweet of fruit. If you have weakness accompanied by constipation, add black sesame to your diet and cook it into a porridge with rice. For a quicker or easier option, have tahini on toast. If you have weakness and often have diarrhoea or loose stools, skip the sesame seeds and use barley or millet. Yin deficiency signs are red cheeks and tongue, hot palms and soles, night sweats and afternoon fevers, and frequent, small thirst.

If the deficiency is specific to the liver yin, signs will include dizziness, dry eyes and weak vision, night blindness, ringing in the ears and dry, brittle nails. Emotionally, deficient liver yin can manifest as depression, nervous tension or irritability. On the other hand, balanced liver yin nurtures, calms and stabilises. Having a strong liver yin protects against excess yang symptoms. Foods that boost liver yin include soybean products, millet and liver. While eating liver is too strong for some people in spring, a yin deficiency is a good reason to eat liver.

Blood and the liver

Without sufficient blood production in the body, possible problems include anaemia, numbness, pale fingernail beds and face, memory loss, insomnia and seeing spots in front of the eyes. Without enough blood stored in the liver, you may experience weak tendons and sinews, muscle spasms and palpitations, spots in your visual field, dry eyes and unclear vision, pale fingernail beds, ringing in the ears and irregular periods or very light or absent periods. Emotionally, insufficient blood can cause depression, nervous tension or irritability. Watercress is a spring food that builds yin and blood.

Water is yin and oil is yang. Cooking food in water promotes yin and is good for anyone who has a yang excess, such as people with high cholesterol or high blood pressure (indicated by a reddish tongue).

•

Buy oils that come in dark glass. Light and heat can turn oils rancid, which means they will do more harm than good.

•

Cooking quickly with direct heat and a very small amount of water retains vegetable freshness. Cooking over a longer time on low heat makes vegetables sweeter and more warming.

•

A small amount of the sour flavour is calming if you are in a fury, but too much will cause stagnation and injure digestion.

•

If liver yin is very deficient, menstruation may stop. If yang is excessive, periods may be very heavy, draining the essence of the kidneys. Use food to build yin and calm yang.

Women wanting to get pregnant can improve their chances by making sure their blood is flowing strongly. A healthy blood flow will also help anyone who is too thin, feels occasional numbness in the hands and feet or has dry skin and hair or a pale face. Eat plenty of leafy greens, Chinese red dates, beans and peanuts and small amounts of liver and red meat.

Liver yang excess

To be balanced, organs need to hold the middle ground and be neither deficient nor excessive. Too much strength overwhelms the body's other organs and systems, but weakness means the organ is unable to fulfil its function and support the other organs. Each organ has a tendency to go one way or the other in its most sensitive season. The liver is often excessive in spring.

The liver is a real action organ. It gives you force and helps you to get things done. But too much liver yang or qi can manifest as anger. So liver yang is like rain – without any rain, nothing grows, with the right amount of rain, things thrive and with vast quantities of rain, everything is washed away.

Foods that calm the liver will benefit everyone during spring. For people who have plenty of yang characteristics, or heat, this is even more relevant. Sweet foods – that's the full sweetness of grains, vegetables and meat – soothe aggressive liver emotions such as anger and impatience. In spring, foods such as bay leaf, coconut milk, black sesame, celery, kelp and spring onions all have a calming effect on the liver qi. These can be particularly useful, since if the liver qi gets out of hand, it can invade the spleen causing vomiting, nausea, distension, flatulence and diarrhoea. As long as there are no signs of heat, quick-acting sweeteners can be eaten in spring to calm the liver. Try raw honey, apple cider vinegar or liquorice root.

In spring, since the liver is likely to be in excess, there is a need to stimulate the liver only very gently. As one of the most stimulating foods for the liver, eating liver should generally be avoided in spring, as it can increase liver strength making its action excessive and causing an imbalance amongst the internal organs. This is especially true if you have a strong and vigorous body type, or if you have a history of aggressiveness.

Vertigo (in someone with a red face), splitting headaches and conjunctivitis may be symptoms of a yang-yin imbalance in the liver where yang is in excess. These health issues are most likely to occur in middle age. Foods that cool and calm liver yang can be useful. Try celery, watercress, lettuce and seaweed. If these are new foods to your diet, introduce them slowly and don't overeat them as they can cause diarrhoea.

Overeating and how it affects the liver

Eating a lot of greasy food tends to make the liver work harder, which puts it into overdrive and increases the likelihood it will be out of balance with the spleen and therefore cause damage to the spleen. And when these two organs are out of balance, the control cycle backfires and the liver attacks the spleen rather than controlling it. The attack on the spleen harms digestion – the spleen will be more likely to turn nutrients into fat rather than into muscle or it will not absorb the nutrients at all.

Over eating, especially of rich, greasy foods, makes the liver work so hard, it gets sluggish, and then it can't distribute qi properly. The qi then stagnates in the liver. When qi and fluids don't flow about the body

and tendons suffer. Tendons can tear, become inflamed or
s may become red, itchy or swollen or they may develop
abnormalities such as cataracts.

Another thing to consider to support the spleen and not aggravate the liver is that if food is too squashed in the stomach (which can be caused by overeating or poor posture), there is no room for the digestion process to take place. When food has nowhere to go, it becomes sludge and all the organs miss out on the nutrients that were in the food, regardless of how fresh or beneficial it could have been.

The onset of puberty can cause stomach fire. While this is sometimes limited in winter because of the cold, it can be exacerbated in spring. Too much greasy and spicy food increases heat rising from the stomach. Combined with overeating, this causes excess mucus production which leads to acne, emotional instability and hot-headedness.

If you habitually overeat and struggle with excess weight, focus on what you can eat rather than on what you can't eat. This may remove some of the desperation from your eating patterns. Use bitter and pungent flavours, such as turnips, to encourage weight loss. Mung beans can also be helpful if you are trying to lose weight. Although they are sweet, mung beans have a cooling, drying, diuretic effect that is useful, particularly if you are showing signs of cold, such as a white tongue. For anyone with cold symptoms, mung beans can do more damage than good. Rye and oats may also assist with weight loss. Or try the pungency of basmati rice. Corn is a useful diuretic if used sparingly so that it does not hurt digestion. Another way to reduce moisture in the body is with foods that increase urination such as adzuki beans and celery.

When the liver becomes sluggish

Stagnant liver qi, which in many cases is caused by overeating, means the qi is blocked and can cause feelings of 'sluggishness'. This leads to anger and frustration and a sense of being held back. At first, if the liver qi becomes blocked we can become depressed or frustrated, and then when the qi pushes through the blockage all at once, it shows up as anger. In a physical sense, liver stagnation can cause a sensation of having a lump in the throat or neck, distension in the breasts or abdomen, or clotting during menstruation.

Other stagnant liver signs include allergies, lumps or swelling, chronic indigestion, neck and back tension, fatigue, an inflexible body, eye problems, skin disorders, fingernail or toenail problems, muscular pain, tendon problems and being slow to get going in the morning. Emotional signs of stagnancy can be emotional repression, anger, frustration, resentment, impatience, edginess, depression, moodiness, impulsiveness, poor judgement, difficulty making decisions, mental rigidity and negativity.

The liver is the storage and purification centre for blood. It releases extra blood for menstruation or for increased activity levels. If the liver qi is stagnant, the blood purification duties of the liver will suffer and toxins may be released into the blood stream. These toxins may eventually show up as acne, eczema or other skin problems. Blood toxins will also make degenerative problems, such as arthritis, worse.

Foods that help ease liver stagnancy in spring include both pungent and sweet foods. Try watercress, cardamom, oregano, dill, pepper or rosemary. In some cases, where the stagnancy is partly due to weakness in the liver rather than overwork, there may not be enough of the sour flavour in the diet. However it's important to add sour foods very gradually, otherwise you can become constipated or get very tight tendons that may cause pain and injury. If you feel nervous and depressed or a bit frustrated, sour foods should help.

The term 'gung-ho' comes
from the Chinese term for
liver fire, 'gan huo'.

•

Peppermint tea can dispel
wind and heat, clear the
head and eyes and relieve
stagnant qi. Try a cup to
relieve nausea.

•

Stress headaches are
connected to the function
of the liver. They may be
reduced or eliminated by
drinking spearmint tea or
eating celery.

•

Take an interest in the
health of the animals you
eat – their health will affect
yours.

•

Cabbage, broccoli and leafy
greens promote digestion
of meat.

•

If you are nervous or
agitated, improve your
level of calm by garnishing
meals with shallots.

•

Mental depression is
experienced in the mind,
but the source may be a
stagnant liver.

Heat in the liver

If a yang excess continues for a long time, the yang
rises and sends heat upwards through the body,
and the yin becomes overwhelmed. The symptoms can include headaches, vertigo, bloodshot
eyes, insomnia, a red tongue and a flushed face.
The red tongue, bloodshot eyes, headaches
and flushed face are related to the yang excess,
while the vertigo and insomnia are a result of
a yin deficiency. The most common outcome
of this imbalance is hypertension or high blood
pressure.

Rising liver heat can also be caused by stagnancy. In its struggle to keep up with the workload
caused by heavy foods that block liver function, a
stagnant liver eventually generates liver heat,
often called liver fire. Liver heat symptoms
include anger and impatience, headaches and
migraines, dizziness and high blood pressure.
Based on the support and control cycle, the liver
feeds the heart, but when you are angry, the liver
fire feeds the heart fire. Too much fire being fed to
the heart can cause insomnia and, because its
source is anger in the liver, it is the type of insomnia
where you can't stop working things over in your
mind – not even enough to close your eyes.

Other liver heat signs include a red face, red,
dry eyes, red tongue, menopausal disorders, indigestion and constipation. Liver heat can predis-
pose people to frequent irritability, an explosive

personality, shouting, wilfulness, arrogance, rudeness, aggression and even violence. To cool liver heat, the kidneys, which are the mother of the liver, need to build up yin fluids. If the liver heat continues, and the kidneys have to over-produce for an extended period, then the kidney yin function will become weakened. Watercress is a good food to cool and detoxify the liver in spring. And because watercress also builds yin, it is perfect to counteract heat in the liver. Bitter and sour foods help to reduce liver excess, too. Try grapefruit, rye or chamomile. With signs of liver heat, use sour foods to calm the immediate symptoms, such as feelings of anger, rather than as a regular part of the diet during spring.

Organ interaction – how they work together in spring

As we've seen, the zang organs are both dependent on and supporting of each other. The liver is supported or fed by the kidneys, while it supports or feeds the heart. The mother–child relationship between the liver as mother and the heart as child is harmed by stagnancy in the liver. The heart doesn't receive the support it needs from the liver which, over time, can lead to heart problems.

If the liver is over-zealous and stronger than the other organs, it will steal too much strength from the kidneys, weakening them, and it can overfeed and unbalance the heart with too much fire. However, if the heart is very strong, it can channel the fire and create more happiness – the emotion linked to the heart. By specifically strengthening the heart with food (which would naturally be done in summer), the heart will not accept the liver excess, so joy and compassion can build up. It all depends on the balance between the organs. If the heart isn't strong, the liver excess causes harm, but a strong heart can resist the extra force of the liver. However, this extra force may then attack the spleen.

Normally, when the organs are balanced, the control cycle works to keep them that way. The lungs control the liver, and the liver controls the

Fish are much harder to catch in windy conditions, and can be scarce in spring. 'Tis the season to enjoy scallops, prawns and calamari.

•

Chinese red dates (da zao or jujubes) act as a sedative and calm the mind and spirit. Make a meal of them by adding a few to rice congee. They are an excellent support for the spleen during spring.

•

Many young people are studying for exams in spring. Eat simple, slowly cooked meals with only a few ingredients. This encourages deep, clear thought.

•

People engaged in a lot of physical activity create more internal warmth and can eat more raw foods, such as salads, during the warmer months. If you are weak or deficient or not very active, stick to warm, freshly cooked foods as much as possible.

•

To relieve tired sore eyes, try tea made from chrysanthemum flowers.

spleen. However, the control cycle can become one of destruction. If an organ becomes excessive, instead of controlling the next organ it attacks it. If the liver becomes too strong, it attacks the spleen and can ignore the limiting force of the lungs.

If the spleen qi is deficient, it means the spleen is unable to defend itself against an excessive liver, and digestion is harmed. Some of the symptoms include weakness, fatigue and loose stools. Over time this can lead to food allergies, anaemia, weakness in the arms and legs, or chronic diarrhoea. In spring, be sure to eat foods to strengthen the spleen against attack from the liver. Try chick peas, parsnip and peas. Carrots and peas also harmonise the relationship between the stomach and the spleen, which improves digestion. If you already have a spleen weakness in the form of damp, be sure to eat plenty of foods that remove damp. This will also support the spleen against attack. Try broad beans, rye, Job's tears barley, tuna, and herbs such as cardamom, cinnamon, turmeric and pepper. While rye is an excellent dryer of damp, it can be a little hard on the digestion system if your spleen is weak. If you already have several symptoms of spleen weakness, eat rye sparingly.

Qi flows through our organs and body in specific patterns that support us. However, if we get out of balance, qi can become rebellious, which means it flows against its normal pattern. The liver might attack the spleen instead of pushing the blood, thereby harming digestion. Causes of rebellious qi in the liver can include emotional upset, spicy food or too much alcohol. Ulcers, haemorrhoids and migraines can be connected to rebellious liver qi.

Looking after the gallbladder

The rich, fatty foods that make the liver struggle also have a negative impact on the gallbladder, which can manifest as indigestion, flatulence, shoulder tension and a bitter taste in the mouth. Remember that spring is the time for energy to float up and anything heavy, such as oil or rich foods, weigh us down and make it very difficult for energy to move up. A simple diet of cooked vegetables, grains and legumes can assist to gradually clear these symptoms. Specific foods that will speed up the process include lemons, limes, turmeric, parsnips, radishes, linseed oil, chamomile tea and seaweed.

So, what to eat in spring?

Foods that eliminate wind, get the energy up and moving. They support liver yin, calm liver yang, remove heat and stagnation from the liver and support the spleen.

In general, foods that are good for spring are warm and ascending sweet foods. In early spring, try cabbage, sweet potato, carrot and beetroot. As the weather changes, move to mint, sweet rice, shiitake mushrooms, peas, sunflower seeds, pine nuts and in late spring, cherries.

Gently warming pungent foods are particularly good for spring. These include fennel (while the weather is still chilly), oregano, rosemary, caraway, dill, bay leaf, grains, legumes and seeds. Pungent flavoured foods stimulate circulation of qi and blood, moving energy up and out. But remember, a little goes a long way. Pungents also regulate qi, enhance

In spring, get rid of phlegm with papaya.

•

For a dry cough, try eating celery.

•

Honey and mint tea is perfect for spring as it is gently warming and encourages qi upwards.

•

To relieve high blood pressure, juice seven stalks of celery and drink.

•

Mung beans, green peas and green beans are colour coordinated to enliven the spirit of spring. They also remove heat, which can be very beneficial for many people during spring.

•

Slippery foods such as honey and spinach should be avoided if you are experiencing slippery conditions such as diarrhoea.

digestion, disperse mucus, stimulate the lungs, blood and heart, guard against mucus-forming conditions such as the common cold, remove obstructions and improve sluggish liver function. Pungents improve digestion and expel flatulence from the intestines to fix bloating. And pungents make grains, legumes, nuts and seeds less mucus forming. Pungent foods you can add to your meals in spring include mint, spring onions, ginger, horseradish, chamomile and black pepper.

Combining foods well can get the best out of them. Spinach strengthens both the blood and the liver, but if you are feeling angry, too much spinach may stimulate the liver and increase your anger. However, spinach can be balanced with tofu, as tofu will counteract the spinach's effect on the liver because tofu builds yin and is cooling. In early spring, you can balance the liver-heating effect of spinach with the very cooling effect of tofu, and offset the tofu (which, if not cooked properly, is so cooling as to be harmful to many people in winter) with a little roast pork. In late spring, especially if you're a hot type, you'll be able to cook the spinach and tofu without the pork. This way, you get the benefits of all the ingredients without putting your body out of balance.

Spring recipes

Spring remedy for the common cold

When a cold is just starting, it's possible – on the first day – to stop it in its tracks before it gains strength.

3 spring onions, white parts only, coarsely chopped
2 slices ginger, 20-cent piece size
2 sprigs mint

Use only the white part of the spring onions near the roots, crush the ginger and add both to two cups of boiling water. Bring back to the boil and simmer uncovered until the liquid content has halved. Add mint, re-boil briefly and drink as soon as it's cool enough. Then hop into bed covering yourself warmly to enhance sweating and sweat the cold out. As soon as the sweating stops, change your bed-wear and bedding so that you don't get sick from being wet and cold. Take it easy for the rest of the day. Be gentle on yourself for the next couple of days, including eating well and getting enough sleep.

Broad bean dip

Broad beans are sweet and strengthen the spleen. Protecting the spleen against an overactive liver in spring is often useful. Broad beans help the body get rid of excess fluids, so can be helpful for people trying to lose weight or who have a continually runny nose.

1 kg of broad beans, shelled

1 clove garlic, crushed

1 teaspoon fresh marjoram

1 teaspoon ground cumin

100 ml extra virgin oil

pinch of salt

black pepper

GARNISH

1 teaspoon of paprika

$^1/_2$ teaspoon of ground cumin

1 tablespoon of extra virgin olive oil

3 chives, chopped

Boil broad beans for ten minutes or until cooked. Drain off half the water and reserve for later. Put beans and the water into a blender. Add garlic, marjoram, cumin, oil, salt and pepper. Blend. You may need to add more of the reserved water if the mixture looks too thick. Blend again, then place in the middle of a large plate. For the garnish, mix herbs and oil, and drizzle over bean mix. Top with chives. Serve with flat mountain bread.

Asparagus soup

Asparagus supports the heart, lungs, spleen and kidneys. Asparagus is calming and its yin-supporting qualities are enhanced by consuming it in the form of soup. Asparagus helps balance fluids and gets rid of excess moisture while moisturising dryness. Adding pepper, thyme and onion to this soup counteracts the slightly cold effect of asparagus, making the meal balanced.

50 g butter

2 sprigs thyme

1 onion, chopped

2 potatoes, scrubbed and finely chopped

500 g asparagus

pinch of salt

black pepper

extra thyme, chopped

sour cream, optional

In a large saucepan, melt the butter and sauté thyme, onion and potatoes for five minutes. Add a litre of water, cover and simmer until the potatoes are thoroughly cooked. Meanwhile, break off the tough ends of the asparagus. Cut off the tips of eight asparagus spears and put them aside. Finely chop remaining asparagus and, with salt, add to main saucepan when potatoes are cooked. Boil rapidly for five minutes. Boil the eight spears in a separate saucepan for five minutes, then drain. Puree contents of the main saucepan and put through a strainer to remove fibres from the asparagus. Add two spears, pepper, chopped thyme and a small dash of sour cream to each bowl of soup. Serve.

Steamed fish with ginger

Choose whichever fish looks the freshest at the fishmongers. Its size will dictate how many this dish will feed. Sesame oil is very useful in spring because it adds taste without making a meal too spicy. Sesame supports both the liver and kidneys, and may balance symptoms such as vertigo and dizziness, and may improve the health and appearance of the hair and eyes.

pinch of salt

1 mild-flavoured fresh fish with scales, head and guts removed

1 knob ginger, finely shredded

1 generous handful chopped spring onions

1 generous handful chopped coriander

2 teaspoons olive oil or sesame oil

Rub the salt lightly over both sides of the fish and cover the upper side with a layer of shredded ginger. In a steamer, heat water to a rolling boil and place fish on a rack in the steamer. Cover, and steam for up to ten minutes depending on the size of the fish (one minute per 30 grams). If the fish has been in a dish instead of on a rack, tip out any liquid that has gathered in the dish. Sprinkle spring onions and coriander liberally over fish and drizzle warm olive oil or sesame oil on top.

French-style green peas

This dish, with its cooked lettuce, may be helpful for both high blood pressure and for removing damp and heat from the body.

2 carrots, finely sliced

1 spring onion, chopped

3 outer leaves lettuce, finely sliced

1 teaspoon butter

300 g shelled peas

Place carrots, spring onion, lettuce and butter in a saucepan and cover. Heat on moderate for five minutes. Add peas and two tablespoons of water. Cover and simmer for seven minutes. Serve with STEAMED FISH WITH GINGER.

Scallops with asparagus

SERVES 2

Chilli and garlic can clear damp, which is indicated by a sticky white coating on the tongue.

$^3/_4$ cup rice

10 asparagus spears

1 teaspoon butter

300 g fresh scallops

3 tablespoons olive oil

1 mild chilli, finely chopped

1 clove garlic, finely chopped

Cook the rice using the absorption method. Remove the woody ends of the asparagus and steam in lightly salted water. When cooked, brush with butter. Cut off scallop intestines (the small fatty line that may contain some black). Heat oil in a wok or frying pan and add chilli and garlic to hot oil. Sauté for one to two minutes. Add scallops and cook for one minute. Serve the asparagus on a bed of rice and top with the scallops.

The absorption method: rinse uncooked rice until water runs clear. Drain. Choose a heavy-based pan. Add rice and enough water to cover it by two centimetres. Cover with a tight-fitting lid and bring to a boil. Reduce heat to as low as possible and cook for 20 minutes. Remove the pan from the heat, remove the lid and fluff rice with a fork before serving.

Stir-fried rice noodles with vegetables

SERVES 2

Seasonal vegetables with rice are a nutritious standard in any season. Rice is a good spleen supporter, which is especially important in spring. Sesame oil is strengthening and calming for the liver, and also helps reduce the effects of wind. Broccoli is good for early spring, but later in the season you can substitute it with snow peas or spinach (add at the last minute or two of cooking). Mushrooms support digestion and calm the spirit and the body.

pinch of salt

250 g rice noodles

1 cup sliced mushrooms

2 tablespoons sesame oil

1 cup broccoli, florets

1 cup bean shoots

1 tablespoon shoyu (or any naturally brewed soy sauce)

1 tablespoon extra sesame oil

Fill a large saucepan to the three-quarter mark with water, add salt and bring to a rolling boil. Add noodles, bring back to boil. Boil until done. 'Done' will depend on the noodles – to check, remove a piece and cut. If colour and consistency are even inside and out, the noodles are done. Drain and rinse under cold running water.

As noodles are cooking, sauté mushrooms in sesame oil in a wok for three minutes, add broccoli and sauté for four minutes. When noodles are ready, add them to the wok with the bean shoots, shoyu and extra oil and stir all ingredients together for a minute or two. Serve immediately.

Shiitake mushrooms with tofu

SERVES 4

Shiitake mushrooms are good for the stomach, blood and energy. Peas are an excellent toner for the spleen in spring. Peas also help qi to move in the appropriate direction – and ease hiccups and coughing. People who are cold or deficient may need to add ginger to this meal.

3 dried shiitake mushrooms
1 tablespoon sesame oil
1 cup green peas
1 carrot, grated
pinch of salt
1 cake tofu
dash tamari (or any naturally brewed soy sauce)

Soak mushrooms in a cup of water for 20 minutes. Drain, but keep the water. Finely chop mushrooms then sauté in sesame oil in a wok for two minutes. Add peas and carrot and sauté for a further two minutes. Add $1/3$ of a cup of reserved water (from mushroom soaking) and salt. Cover and cook for 20 minutes. Put tofu and $1/3$ of a cup of reserved water through the blender or mash with a fork. Add tofu and tamari to wok and cook for five minutes. Serve with rice.

Vegetarian shish kebabs

SERVES 6

Tempeh is a cooked soybean patty. It is very strengthening, so is particularly good for anyone who is weak or deficient, although be sure to steam tempeh if you are deficient, as frying could overwhelm a weak digestive system, especially in spring. Tempeh's savoury flavour makes it popular with meat-eaters who are trying to cut down their meat intake.

24 cubes tempeh

12 small mushrooms

12 pieces capsicum

12 small white onions

12 broccoli florets

12 cubes carrot

wooden skewers, soaked in water

BASTING SAUCE

$^1/_2$ cup tamari

1 tablespoon arrowroot

1 tablespoon lemon juice

1 piece grated ginger

splash of mirin

Lightly steam tempeh and vegetables. For the basting sauce, combine all the ingredients and mix well. Marinate the steamed vegetables in the basting sauce for 30 minutes. Place two pieces of tempeh and one piece of each vegetable on each skewer. Brush with sauce and place under grill for two minutes. Baste again, turn over and put back under grill. Continue grilling and basting until cooked according to your preference.

Chicken and rice casserole with prawns

SERVES 4

Chicken and prawns both encourage the body's energy upwards, which is
perfect for spring as it strengthens the body after the cold months of winter.
Ginger with prawns removes wind, which is the element most likely to
infiltrate the body during spring. However, this dish is not appropriate for
people who have excessive heat in the upper body with symptoms such as a
very red face, bloodshot eyes, a skin rash or an acne breakout.

12 dried chestnuts, soaked overnight and drained

250 g chicken

1 teaspoon olive oil

1 cup white rice

16 prawns (uncooked, fresh or frozen) with veins, heads and shells removed

2–3 slices fresh ginger

12 morel mushrooms, sliced

dash shoyu

dash sesame oil

Preheat oven to 190°C. Cut chicken into bite-sized pieces and in a frying
pan lightly sauté in olive oil until chicken is sealed on the outside but
undercooked in the middle. Put aside. Wash rice in cold water, twice. Put
rice in a large casserole dish and cover with water triple the depth of the rice.
Add the chicken and all other ingredients, except shoyu and sesame oil. Stir
together and cover. Bake in oven for 45 minutes. Stir in shoyu and sesame
oil and serve.

CHAPTER FIVE

Summer and its recipes

Summer is a yang season, a time for expansion, with energy moving up and out with a lively brightness. We can make the most of the warm weather and long days by going with the flow of the seasonal conditions. This can be done by eating foods that promote energy and activity, and by balancing summer heat with cooling foods. Take advantage of all the different foods that are available in summer. It's the time to get as much variety into the diet as possible because that is what nature encourages in summer, the perfect time for spices, flowers and leaves that have floating or outward energy.

Heat

Heat in the environment and in the body is common in summer. Inside us, heat behaves much as you might expect it to. Heat rises and dries moisture, and causes us to seek sources of cold.

Many summer foods are brightly coloured and can be cooked using high heat for a short time to promote activity.

•

Sweating can open the pores to release heat, but it means we lose more qi or nutrients in summer, so it is important to eat widely to replace lost nutrients and keep up fluids.

•

Understand and accept that a food is good for you and, when you eat it, its effect will be even better.
– Professor Lun Wong

•

Aim for warm feet and a cool head.

•

Cooking methods affect the internal temperature of food. Frying tends to make food hotter, whereas steaming tends to have a cooling effect.

•

When cooking mung beans, you can counteract their very cold nature by adding black pepper, ginger or cumin for the last 30 minutes of cooking.

Some of the signs of excessive heat include a red face or red eyes or a bright red tongue with either no coating or a yellow coating. Health issues that can appear because of heat include heat exhaustion, fever, high blood pressure, acne, skin eruptions, nosebleeds, constipation, thick or yellow mucus or phlegm, headaches, irritability, excessive sweating, shortness of breath, or wheezing.

Qi is our body's energy and a source of warmth. Qi flows around the body and between organs providing energy for sustenance and function. If an organ becomes too strong, it generates heat and sends out too much qi. The heat from an organ may send qi in the wrong direction or the qi may create heat if there is a blockage. If qi gets blocked, it keeps trying to move. This movement in a small area causes more heat.

In summer, some people experience heart fire because of the heat. A lot of dreaming, restlessness and insomnia indicates an imbalance between the kidney yin and heart. Check the tip of the tongue. If it is red, there is too much heart fire. To clear the heart fire, cook mung bean soup or a mung bean dessert with rock sugar. Mung beans have a very strong cold energy, so it is important not to eat them too regularly. Check your tongue, if the tip isn't red anymore, you've had enough mung beans and you'll be able to sleep more easily. Another way to cut down heart fire and reduce heat is to make a soup with lettuce and small pieces of fish. Add lettuce to rapidly boiling water for one minute – so the lettuce won't be bitter. In summer, only add ginger to meals if there are no signs of heat. Avoid ginger if you have a red tongue with a yellow coating.

Some foods, including red meat and chicken, increase heat in the body so only small portions of these are best in summer. Foods that reduce heat include zucchini, citrus fruits, soy products and kelp.

Especially in summer, red skin rashes usually occur in people who have yang qi congested in the exterior of the body just under the skin. The red of the rash indicates the condition is heat-based, so avoid warm and hot foods that thrust qi outwards, such as chicken, prawns, lobster, mussels, spicy or fried foods, peanuts and alcohol.

Heat can also affect the stomach qi by forcing it up (naturally, stomach qi flows down). Acidic regurgitation is one example of rebellious qi. Anything fried will make rebellious qi worse because frying makes all foods warmer or more yang. When the stomach qi moves in the wrong direction, bitter foods can be used to push it down again. Actually, the bitter herbs affect the heart rather than the stomach, but once the heart qi moves down, it leads the stomach qi down too. Another option is to use sinking foods such as seaweed.

Damp

Dampness in the body is always to do with the spleen and it may be exacerbated by the environment in late summer. Since the spleen is responsible for transforming and transporting nutrition that enters the stomach, how the spleen is functioning will have a pivotal affect on what the body does with what you eat. If the digestive system is working poorly, some of the food and drink that has been consumed will not be digested properly and will be left to stagnate. Over time, this stagnant mess forms damp and phlegm, and deposits itself around the body.

While damp can be caused by eating the wrong foods, even the right foods can cause damp if you overeat. If food is jammed into the stomach too tightly, there is no room for the digestive juices to do their job, so the contents of the stomach can't be digested fully. The digestive system works harder and harder. The extra effort overheats the stomach and causes the spleen to create more dampness.

Heat in the stomach is a sensation connected with hunger. So, even if the last meal hasn't been properly digested, you may feel hungry and eat again. This puts more pressure on the digestive system which fills with more and more stagnant food. Undigested liquid can block the functions of the spleen, and when this liquid mixes with stagnant food it forms phlegm. And more heavy sludge gathers. Over time, the weight of the dampness pushes down where it gathers around the kidneys and liver. Since the kidneys are a major support for the stomach and spleen, what slows and hinders kidney function also harms the stomach and spleen.

Damp makes people feel tired and sluggish and heavy. Unlike wind, dampness keeps pain in one place. Dampness can manifest as oedema, excessive weight, mucus, cysts or plaque. Bitter foods are useful to help remove damp. Try celery, rye, asparagus and lettuce, although these should be eaten only in small amounts by anyone who is weak or deficient. If there are signs of heat as well (such as a yellow coating on the tongue) try peppermint, chamomile or radish.

Damp around the kidneys can cause urinary tract infections. Add a handful of washed corn-silk to 700 ml of boiling water and simmer for ten minutes. Remove the corn-silk and sip the water. In the heart, dampness and mucus can stifle circulation. This can manifest as drooling, sudden movements or talking to yourself.

Depression often occurs when damp turns to phlegm. Phlegm causes everything it surrounds to slow down and become clouded. The effects can include dizziness, poor memory and concentration, feeling numb or being unable to express emotion.

The organs of summer

The yin–yang, zang–fu organs of summer are the heart and small intestine and, later in the season, the spleen and stomach. The heart's physical function is controlling blood circulation and the blood vessels, however, it plays central roles on other levels too. The heart controls consciousness, sleep and memory and provides a haven for the spirit, or shen.

Shen is the TCM term for spirit and mind. It is a yang energy and is based in the heart. Within the heart, shen is balanced by heart yin. If the shen is stable and the heart balanced, you will be friendly and open to the world. People with healthy hearts are very aware of the world around them without being overwhelmed by it and they are able to come up with solutions to problems. If the heart yin is not strong, shen escapes from its stable base in the heart and flies to the head, where thoughts rush around uncontrolled. Over time, this causes worry, insomnia, irregular heartbeat or wild dreams. Constant worrying over a long period can lead to deficiency in both the spleen qi and the heart blood.

When the heart is imbalanced, you won't sleep well. Heart fire, which is too much heat in the heart, can push down on

Most foods contain more than one flavour, but the refining process removes other flavours from refined sweets. Refined sugars aren't balanced by other flavours so, if taken in excess, they go directly to the spleen and send it into overdrive. This creates more dampness, and ultimately more fat.

•

Fat tissue is mostly phlegm and dampness, so to control and then eliminate excess fat, you need to eat foods that promote the stomach and spleen during digestion, strengthen the kidneys and dry damp.

•

The spleen and stomach work best with a diet of warm-natured, freshly cooked, non-fatty foods, eaten warm. Cold and raw foods and drinks make the stomach work hard to warm its contents before digestion can start.

•

The spirit rules the qi, so how your energy manifests in the world directly correlates with your spirit.

When the heart is serene,
pain seems negligible.
– *Nei Jing*

•

In the Ayurvedic medicine
of India, the chakras
represent the energy core
running through the centre
of the body. Different herbs
support the various chakras
– the heart is helped by
herbs such as saffron and
rose. In Western cultures,
roses are the flowers to win
a heart.

•

If spleen qi is blocked from
moving up, or stomach qi is
blocked from moving down
after eating, there's no
room for digestion.
Undigested food creates
dampness and mucus that,
over time, inhibit all the
body's organs and
activities.

•

Bloating and pain during
menstruation is often due
to damp and cold, so even
in summer it makes sense
to support the spleen with
warm, cooked foods
especially before and
during menstruation.

the stomach and affect the digestion system, including the spleen and the appetite. Then the stomach catches the fire from the heart. Stomach fire causes stomach qi to move up, instead of down to eliminate waste. With the heart (the mother) feeding fire to both the spleen and the stomach (the children), the stomach pushes the heat upwards to the face, making it red.

Imbalances of the heart can lead to a scattered, confused mind, either too much or no laughter, a very red or very pale face, speech problems such as a stutter or verbal diarrhoea, depression, mental illness, loss of memory, poor circulation, a weak spirit, or an aversion to heat.

The health of the heart shows up in our facial complexions. The emotions directly related to the heart are happiness and joy, which can also manifest as self-awareness. Check the general condition of the whole tongue because the heart opens to the tongue and the tip of the tongue. According to TCM, the heart is the organs' leader and the body's central organ. However, the best way to support and treat the heart with diet is often indirectly, through either calming or supporting other organs that may be out of balance. This is one more reason to eat as widely as you can in summer.

The spleen and stomach are essential and sensitive in every season of the year. However, in late summer and during the changeover between seasons, it is a good opportunity to pay this zang–fu pair some extra attention. The stomach only deals with digestion. While spleen qi moves up, stomach qi moves down to eliminate waste from the body. When stomach qi rebels and moves up it can cause vomiting or burping. The spleen has several functions. First, its qi moves nutrients up to the heart to create blood, and up to the lungs to create the body's protective qi. And the spleen controls and directs digestion. The spleen likes dryness, but if the digestive system becomes too dry the result is constipation. But if the spleen is weakened by dampness, or stressed by the wrong foods or too much food, it creates more dampness that weakens it further. Problems that can be experienced by someone with excessive damp in the body include being overweight, general heaviness, oily skin or phlegm.

Anxiety, worry and obsession are all linked to the spleen and can harm the digestive process and the spleen's role in creating blood and immunity. This can manifest in the body as poor digestion, flabbiness, chronic tiredness, nausea, insensitive taste buds, loose stools or undigested food in the stool, abdominal distension, poor appetite and blood-sugar imbalances. There is also a tendency to have a sloppy appearance and accumulate things. A healthy spleen and digestive system encourages people to be practical, caring, self-reliant and creative.

The health of the spleen shows up in our appearance in several ways. The most obvious is the flesh. When the spleen is working well and not being over-burdened, the spleen creates muscle. Alternatively, if the spleen is struggling, fat is created, even though you may not be eating excessively. The lips are another indicator of the state of the spleen. They should be soft and supple, without being dry or peeling. Another minor function of the spleen is to ensure the blood stays within the blood vessels. If you bruise very easily, the spleen isn't as strong as it could be and could do with some pampering.

The flavours of summer – bitter and sweet

Bitter and sweet are the flavours of summer. They are connected to the heart and spleen respectively. Bitter is yin, cooling, descending and contracting. It reduces excesses such as heat, and dries and drains dampness. Bitter eases inflammations and infections. Bitter reduces swelling and encourages bowel movements so is good news for people trying to lose weight, especially for people with a red tongue, indicating heat. Internal heat can be eased with the bitter flavour during any season of the year. For the heart, bitter clears heat and removes damp and mucus in the arteries, which helps lower blood pressure. For the liver, bitter removes stagnancy and clears heat. However, the descending and cooling nature of bitter means it shouldn't be overdone in summer unless you have a lot of fire. Bitter foods include dandelion, yarrow, chamomile, alfalfa, bitter melon, lettuce and rye. Asparagus, celery, lettuce and papaya are bitter and sweet.

Sweet is yang, moves up and out and is linked to the spleen. Sweet foods build and strengthen the spleen and ultimately the entire body. They provide energy and, simultaneously, have a slowing and relaxing effect, build the yin (tissues and fluids) and alleviate weakness and deficiency. Sweet flavours have a calming and strengthening effect on the brain and nerves. Sweet slows an overactive heart and mind, soothes aggressiveness and eases impatience. The sweet flavour encourages the digestive system to produce fluid, which it needs for digestion.

While sweet foods provide the spleen with qi, too much sweetness weakens the spleen instead of strengthening it, because excessive sweet causes dampness. Refined sweets, such as sugar, are very sweet and if you eat a lot of them, the stomach will overproduce fluid that then harms the spleen and its function. Later, the excess fluid becomes damp that causes blockages and is difficult for the body to expel. Once the spleen is overwhelmed, it becomes weak, and starts to crave sweet, simply because sweet was the flavour that in small amounts gave the spleen qi. As the spleen demands, and then gets more sweet food, the damage level rises and the cravings intensify. It follows that the sweeter a food, the more likely it is to create damp and create or heighten a destructive sugar dependence. Sweet foods also cause energy to rise. Too much pushes all the energy into the upper part of the body and leaves the lower body deficient. But the nutritional value of sweet foods is both essential and beneficial. Sweet foods include oats, rice, peaches, beef, avocado, peas, kiwifruit and cucumber.

People who are very active in summer and sweat a lot will need to eat salty foods occasionally, which will calm the pulse and are good for the skin in summer. Sour foods will help to balance the liver. Bitter clears heart fire. Pungent foods help clear the lungs and balance the liver and heart.

Excesses and blockages

Excess in the body shows you can have too much of a good thing. Too much strength in one area means there is not enough to counterbalance it in another area. Once the body gets out of balance, you will be in some kind of discomfort until balance is restored.

Relaxing will improve digestion, and improving digestion will help you to relax. It doesn't matter which you start with, just start.

•

The bitter flavour of dandelion reduces heat and damp, especially in the heart, liver, spleen and lungs. It can help reduce bladder infection.

•

Too much sweetness can weaken the bones and make the hair fall out.

•

When you have a cough, sweet substances help carry the medicine up into the lungs – which is why cough syrups are so effective. However, too much sweetness should be avoided as it will increase mucus.

•

Some foods, including oats and celery, have a calming effect on hypertension and will be helpful in managing stress.

•

Fatty foods are usually too heavy for summer.

In summer, when the digestive system can be over-heated, use cardamom. Cardamom is especially good for barbecues because it clears the digestive system of blockages caused by heat. As it is 'fired' food, barbecues should be avoided by people with excess heat (indicated by a red and yellow tongue).

•

Heart fire can be caused by fire from liver (the mother–child relationship of support), emotional upset and insomnia (imbalance in the heart itself) or not enough water from the kidneys (kidneys failing to limit the heart).

•

Get rid of summer phlegm with strawberries, string beans or radish. For a dry cough use mangoes or asparagus.

•

During summer (and any time for people who show signs of excess, such as a sturdy build and a ruddy complexion), choose a lighter miso – one that has been fermented for less than 12 months.

Signs of excess include a red complexion, heavy breathing, a loud voice and an extroverted personality. Foods to ease excess include celery, lettuce, asparagus, rye and legumes. Most legumes are drying and diuretic (except soy beans) so are particularly good for excessive types of people.

A common sign of excess linked to the heart is hypertension. Food can help. Try radishes, celery, bananas (avoid banana if you have excess damp), persimmons, seaweed, mung beans, raw honey and hawthorn fruit. Eat legumes without oil and they will improve physical balance, leaving you feeling calm and focused.

Excess can be caused by blockages within the body. The body reacts to blockages by trying to push through the blockage, which causes heat. As blockages are often caused by phlegm or mucus, bitter herbs can be used to reduce heat and blockages because bitter herbs are both cooling and drying.

Dampness, if left for a long time, tends to block energy from flowing within the body. Eventually it causes joint pain and stiffness, such as arthritis, aching knees or tennis elbow. Even though the problem comes from the inside, these will be worse in a damp environment. Foods that help this problem are the same ones that dry and help any damp condition but you can also eat foods that open energy paths inside the body – try black sesame seeds, black soy beans, capers, turnips (in winter), mulberries, dried ginger, Job's tears barley, and pine nuts. Peanuts can make damp worse. Kidneys are in charge of fluids in the body (even though dampness is created by the spleen), so it's important to eat foods that support the kidneys too.

Shortness of breath, chest pain, fatigue or palpitations may indicate mucus blocking the blood flow, which will show up on the tongue as a thick, greasy tongue coat. If there is mucus on and around the heart, it can cause problems such as drooling. If the mucus is hot, it is likely to affect the nervous system and cause erratic sudden movement, whereas if the mucus is cold it can contribute to slower movement and symptoms such as self-obsession and talking to yourself. From a dietary point of view, improving the health of the heart in these cases is the same as clearing damp from the digestive system.

Heart yin deficiency

Many heart problems are deficiencies, especially of the heart yin and blood. One of the first signs of heart yin weakness is thinking that never seems to stop, yet isn't focused. This is because shen isn't anchored in the heart by the yin, and has flown to the head. Deficient heart yin leads to nervousness and stress, whereas a strong heart yin stops the heart getting overheated and inflamed as is the case with hypertension.

Often a lack of yin in the heart is a flow-on effect of a lack of yin in the liver or kidneys (another reason to aim for balance in every season). If yang is too strong in the liver, more liver yin is used up balancing yang. Alcohol, tobacco and coffee are warming substances that may deplete kidney yin, which will have a flow-on effect for the heart. Anything that supports kidney yin (see WINTER AND ITS RECIPES, page 114) will also benefit the heart.

Rice, wheat, oats, cucumber, celery and lettuce calm the mind and strengthen nerve and heart tissue. Mulberries, lemons, jujube, dill, basil and chamomile are calming too. Pungents, such as dill, baby fennel, caraway, anise, cumin and coriander, relax the nervous system. The bitter flavour cleans the heart by clearing heart excesses downwards to be expelled. Bitter foods also cool, and remove liver stagnation, which is important for the heart because of the mother–child relationship.

If there are signs of heat with a yin deficiency, such as night sweats, hot palms and soles, insomnia and continuous but small appetite, then eat more soups with cooling foods such as tofu, mung beans and kelp. Cool pungents, such as peppermint, oregano, elder flowers and radish, may also help people with signs of heat.

Deficient heart blood manifests as a general sluggishness and paleness in the face, nail beds and tongue. The health and vitality of the heart blood is usually related to weaknesses in the kidneys and spleen. Blood is created from nutrients gathered from the digestion process and combined with the jing, which is the kidney essence. Any food that supports the kidneys and allows the spleen to improve function will improve heart blood supplies. Raspberries, eggplant, adzuki beans, chives, nutmeg, mint and basil nourish the blood in summer.

Heart deficiencies of qi and yang

Heart qi directs the flow of fluids and blood through the heart. When it is weak, it can result in palpitations, low energy levels and a pale tongue. In the long-term, qi and yang heart deficiencies can result in hardening and thickening of the arteries (because blood and fluids haven't been moving strongly enough), nervous disorders, general weakness or depression. Because the heart is supported by the liver (through the mother–child relationship) deficiencies in the heart can often be related to stagnation in the liver. Since qi is most likely to get stuck and stagnate in the liver, the qi of the entire body, including the heart qi can be negatively affected by liver stagnation. The heart qi is provided and supported by the lungs and spleen, so heart qi weakness may relate back to these two source organs.

Yang is warm, so a lack of yang usually causes cold. Where heart yang and heart qi are weak, heart blood may be moving very slowly. This can cause shortness of breath, chest pain, fatigue or palpitations. In some cases, the tongue may be purple. If you experience these symptoms, use diet to nourish heart blood and see a health practitioner (see HEART YIN DEFICIENCY, page 61).

When there is too much heart yang, the heart emotions become unbalanced. Hypoglycaemia (low blood sugar), despair, anorexia and insomnia can be a result of an imbalance in the heart. To control imbalances, calm the heart yang with bitter foods, grains, vegetables and legumes.

Supporting the kidneys and liver in summer

The kidneys are pivotal in summer because they support both the digestion process and the heart. The stomach and spleen are known as the middle burner. The middle burner draws much of its strength from the kidneys, so strengthening and toning the kidneys supports digestion. The kidney yin supplies water for the heart which, in the heat of summer, is even more sensitive than usual. Summer foods to nurture the kidney yin include green beans, berries and watermelon.

Anything pushed to the extreme can transform into its opposite. We know extreme cold can 'burn'. Within the body, heat and high blood pressure (yang) can cause stroke and paralysis (yin).

•

If you have a problem with energy and motivation, your kidneys could probably use a boost. Rice with kidney beans and vegetables should help.

•

The chances of conception can be improved by promoting the health of the kidneys – for both men and women. In summer, eat raspberries.

•

Watermelon is known as the 'natural white tiger' because of its heat-clearing properties.

•

When smaller amounts of food are eaten, less qi is used in digestion and therefore you'll have more energy.

•

Even in summer, people with damp should mostly eat cooked meals, but avoid deep-fried foods.

If you are experiencing mood swings or angry outbursts, your liver may require special attention. In summer, foods to reduce liver excess include romaine lettuce, asparagus, alfalfa, mung beans, mulberry, basil, peaches, celery, cucumber, seaweed, tofu and radish. Mild depression or menstrual clotting caused by liver stagnancy may be eased with basil, cherry, coconut milk, eggplant, lychee, oregano, peach, rosemary, safflower, saffron, strawberry, mint and lemon balm. Nervousness, dizziness or itching may be related to wind and can be eased in summer with basil, sage or peppermint. Other sweet and sour foods to benefit the liver in summer include blackberry, huckleberry, raspberry, mango, tomato and yoghurt.

So, what to eat in summer?

Foods that strengthen and support the heart, cool the symptoms of summer heat, nourish the kidneys, boost the spleen and dry damp are the best choices for summer.

The heat of summer makes hard work for the digestive system, so there should be a predominance of light and easy-to-digest foods. Heat producing foods should be eaten only in small amounts. Remember to think about the ingredients in a meal, the season and your own personal needs. For example, meat (especially red meat) is heating within the body. Exercise also generates heat. So, if you are very physically active, have a naturally strong build, already have a meat-dominated diet, and are showing symptoms of heat and excess, it might be best to cut down on red meat. An increase in the amount of fruit, vegetables and grain eaten in summer will help deal with heat and benefit the heart and spleen. Other ways to balance a meat meal are to add cardamom to the cooking process, avoid burning (or direct firing, such as grilling or barbecuing) the meat and include cooling foods in the meal. Alternatively, someone who is thin or weak, or is sensitive to cold, can use summer and warming foods, such as small amounts of beef, to give themselves a boost.

Foods that specifically clear heat during summer include avocado, banana, kiwifruit, mulberry, peach, pineapple, strawberry, watermelon (and other melons), alfalfa, asparagus, barley, celery, crabmeat, cucumber, lettuce, millet, mung beans, peppermint, radish, tofu, tomato, watercress and wheat.

There are some foods that were just made for summer. It is the best time to eat tofu and salads. Tofu is cold, so eating too much when it is cold outside may cool you too much on the inside as well. But in summer, cooling is just what many people need. Even in summer, if you tend to have a lot of cold in your body, try lightly frying tofu in olive oil before adding it to the rest of the dish. Salads are best eaten when the weather is hot but they need to be well-chewed. Since raw foods take more heat and energy to be broken down, consider whether you have energy to spare. Exercise creates more heat in the body, so if you exercise a lot, your digestive system will have more heat. If you have a strong build and show other signs of internal heat, such as a loud voice and a red face, salads will help you during summer as long as you chew thoroughly. However if you are deficient, weak, flabby or very thin, with a

With so many foods available, there's no need to eat the same foods every day – which means you'll need to consider what different foods are made of. If you always eat bread and pasta made from wheat, occasionally consider rye bread or pasta made of corn, buckwheat or rice.

•

Snapper, whiting and flounder are readily available and in great condition during the summer months.

•

When foods are burnt, their nature is changed. Peanuts, which are sweet, become bitter. Beef, which is warm, becomes very hot. It's something to consider when you bring out the barbie in summer.

•

Tofu is an excellent summer food to clear heat. The mineral (gypsum fibrosum) added to soybean juice to create tofu causes the body to lose heat. This is useful if you are have internal heat (a red and yellow tongue) and to be avoided if you are cold or weak (a pale, white-coated tongue).

To barbecue sweet corn in summer, use the natural cover of the cob leaves to protect the sweet corn, although it is best to remove the fine silk from under the leaves before putting the corn onto the heat.

•

Too much eggplant may cause blurred vision.

•

If you grow your own chillies, more water as they grow will make them less hot.

•

TCM attributes the negative impacts of aging to weakened kidneys. Blueberries strengthen kidney yin and summer is their season.

•

Soup is the best cooking medium to nourish the yin which will help balance yang, heat and excess. Choose from the season's vegetables, such as celery, green beans, asparagus, squash, zucchini or sweet corn and add tofu at the end of cooking.

pale tongue or a white tongue coating, it's best not to eat salads with raw or cold vegetables too regularly because they can cause cold and damp within the body. For a more suitable solution, try lightly stir-frying vegetables and adding a little water or stock.

Foods with a bitter flavour support the heart, reduce heat and dry damp. Lettuce, which is bitter and sweet, is a perfect example. Bitter foods tend to direct energy inward and to the lower half of the body, which can be important for people with a yang excess and a depleted yin. Mung beans, cucumber, tofu, millet, seaweed, blackberries and raspberries build yin and blood and guard against handling stress badly or getting run-down or sick. Other foods that support the heart include kidney beans, red lentils and adzuki beans.

If you tend to be dry, moistening foods will help your body deal with summer. The best foods for dry people are the most dampening – bananas, mangoes watermelon and dairy products. When eating legumes, such as lentils or kidney beans, add oil to make them more moistening. Seaweed and salt also help to make a legume dish more moistening if that is what is needed. In countries where legumes are the staple crop, there is a general need to balance this drying – in Mexico with fat and cheese, and in the Middle East with tahini. However, given our varied diet, this won't be necessary for most Australians.

People trying to remove damp can go for kiwifruit, lettuce, asparagus, adzuki beans, rye, alfalfa, oregano, corn and strawberries. As rice has a diuretic affect that expels dampness, it can be eaten without increasing the problem. And since rice supports the spleen, it is particularly helpful for people wanting to remove dampness, which is caused by a weak spleen. Eating well-cooked legumes without much oil or salt will ease water retention and help you feel content and lighter.

Late summer is the transition point between the yang of spring and summer and the yin of autumn and winter. This is when gentle, spleen-supporting foods are on a seasonally aware menu. Nutritional support of the spleen is helpful at every changeover between seasons. Some of the best foods for late summer are those that harmonise the middle burner (stomach and spleen). These include cherries, corn, chickpeas, soybeans, string beans, haricot beans, tofu, strawberries, apricots, peaches, and cantaloupes. And some of the best meals are simple with little seasoning and a small number of ingredients. Keep portions small and chew well.

Summer recipes

Basil and tomato salad

SERVES 4

Basil is both cooling and drying. Its drying quality counteracts the
dampening effect of the bocconcini. There are several sour tastes here,
including the tomatoes, olives and vinegar, which encourages energy down
and enhances the cooling effect. People with damp can lightly grill the
tomatoes, and use less cheese and more basil.

3 cups basil leaves, torn in half

black pepper

$^1/_2$ cup cold-pressed extra virgin olive oil

500 g cherry tomatoes, halved

$^1/_2$ cup black olives, pitted and sliced

6 bocconcini (small white cheeses), sliced

2 teaspoons red-wine vinegar

Put basil, pepper, most of the oil, tomatoes and olives in a large bowl. Put
cheese and remaining oil in another bowl. Add a couple more twists of
pepper. Let everything sit for half an hour. Drain the cheese and place in a
bowl. Add vinegar to the basil and tomato mix, then tip over the bocconcini.
Serve with warm, wholemeal toast.

Bean salad

SERVES 4

String or green beans support the spleen and the digestive system and the kidneys by supplementing yin fluids. The heat of summer can stress the kidneys and bladder, so foods that counteract this are important. Adding yoghurt to beans improves the dish's cooling ability. People with a weak digestive system or damp should cook beans for longer and use less yoghurt. Almonds help clear damp too.

$^1/_2$ kg whole string or green beans

4 lettuce leaves

1 cup natural yoghurt

4 teaspoons fresh sage

1 tablespoon crushed almonds

Lightly steam beans. Arrange lettuce in a bowl. Mix beans and yoghurt, add to bowl. Top with sage and freshly sautéd almonds.

Parsley salad

Parsley is great in summer because of its detoxifying qualities. The heat of summer can allow germs to thrive, so eating parsley is a terrific way to fight germs naturally. Parsley also removes damp and eases most urinary tract problems, helps clear ear infections and gets rid of bad breath. For people feeling oppressed by heat, add more cucumber and use fresh tomatoes. People with damp might choose to forgo the fetta and favour the sun-dried tomatoes instead.

Mix parsley with grilled capsicum, fetta and olives or with butterbeans, cucumber and sun-dried tomatoes. Make your own dressing by mixing olive oil and apple cider vinegar. Let your favourite herbs marinate in the oil and vinegar for half an hour.

Sweet corn soup with crab meat

As they are water-based, soups are good for the body's yin. Corn supports digestion, opens the lungs and settles the heart. Crab can clear heat and boost the body's ability to heal itself, but avoid this dish if you have skin rashes or ulcers.

sesame oil

2 tablespoons finely chopped spring onions

2 slices ginger, finely chopped

250 g picked crab meat

pinch of salt

1 tablespoon rice wine

500 ml chicken stock

4 corn cobs, grated

2 tablespoons shoyu

1 tablespoon cornflour

1 egg

1 tablespoon rice vinegar

Heat one tablespoon of sesame oil in a wok. Sauté spring onion and ginger for one minute. Add crab meat, salt and rice wine. Stir through. Add stock, corn and shoyu, stirring until mixture reaches boiling point. Reduce heat and simmer for three minutes. In a bowl, mix cornflour, two tablespoons of water, a teaspoon of sesame oil and a tablespoon of the soup until smooth. Gently pour the mixture into the soup, stirring constantly. Remove from heat. With a fork, rapidly stir a teaspoon of sesame oil into an egg. Add egg and rice vinegar to the soup. Stir and serve.

Stuffed eggplants

SERVES 4

Red capsicums are the colour of summer. They reduce swelling and distension and promote circulation. Both eggplants and capsicums are good for the digestive system, but avoid eggplant in excessive amounts.

4 eggplants
salt
2 tablespoons olive oil
1 small onion, finely chopped
1 clove garlic
2 red capsicums, chopped
1 bay leaf
1 teaspoon ground cinnamon
3 tablespoons chopped parsley
1 small handful sultanas
juice of a juicy lemon

Cut eggplants in two lengthways. Scoop out flesh, then slice flesh, add the salt and put aside. Salt inside of shells and leave aside. Preheat the oven to 180°C. On the stovetop, in a non-stick pan with one teaspoon of olive oil, sauté onion and garlic, then add capsicum. Cook for two or three minutes. Then add bay leaf, cinnamon and parsley. Cook gently for five more minutes, then tip into a bowl.

Rinse salt from the eggplant flesh and shells. Leave moisture on the flesh but dry the shells. Sauté the eggplant flesh with a tablespoon of oil and a dash of water. Add to the bowl with other cooked ingredients and sultanas, and mix.

Pack mixture into the eggplant shells. Oil a baking dish and brush top of mixture with oil. Make sure the baking dish is small enough so the shells are squished in together for support. Pour a blend of lemon juice and the remaining oil and water into the baking dish so the water comes almost to the tops of the shells. Bake until the eggplants are soft, which will be about 40 minutes.

Eggplant with tomato and basil

SERVES 6

Eggplant's sweet, cooling nature makes it a good choice for a hot summer. The tomatoes and cheese add to this cooling effect. The basil and lemon counteract the dampening effects of the tomato and cheese, while supporting the eggplant's digestion qualities.

3 medium eggplants

salt

1 teaspoon olive oil

1 knob ginger, finely sliced

juice of a lemon

1 tablespoon sesame oil

4 tomatoes, halved

2 large handfuls basil leaves

sourdough rye bread

fetta cheese

Slice eggplants, cover in salt and leave for half an hour. Rinse well and cut into small cubes. Heat wok, add olive oil. When oil is hot, add ginger and sizzle for two minutes. Add eggplant and stir with ginger. Add about half a cup of hot water and cover until eggplant is soft. Remove lid and allow any remaining water to evaporate. Stir to stop the eggplant sticking to the wok. Add lemon juice to eggplant and stir again. Turn off heat and stir in sesame oil. Grill tomato halves, adding basil leaves right before the tomatoes are done. To serve, pile eggplant mix on toasted sourdough rye bread with tomato and basil on the side, lightly sprinkling with fetta cheese.

Stir-fried chicken and tofu with asparagus

SERVES 4

If you have a cold or damp condition or you are overweight, make sure the tofu is thoroughly cooked in a small amount of olive oil before it is added to the stir-fry. Alternatively, the tofu can be replaced with precooked and gently heated adzuki beans.

To improve sluggish digestion, add extra ginger. Or if you have a red tongue with a yellow coating, omit the ginger. People with excessive heat or heart problems, may wish to use less oil and cover the wok or frying pan to create a steaming effect.

olive oil
small knob fresh ginger, finely chopped
1 small onion, finely chopped
4 red capsicums, finely chopped
8 small chicken breast pieces
1 packet firm tofu
shoyu
16 asparagus spears
handful coriander leaves

In a small amount of olive oil, sauté ginger, onion and capsicum. Remove from pan. Making sure the frying pan or wok is very hot, stir-fry chicken pieces. Remove from heat. Mix in the tofu and add a dash of shoyu. Break off the woody ends of the asparagus and steam. Place four spears on each plate as a bed and pile the rest of the ingredients on top. Use the coriander as garnish.

Tempeh with rice

If you struggle keeping weight off, choose white rice over brown because it won't strain your spleen. While it's true that brown rice is more nutritious, it is harder to digest – go easy on yourself if your digestion system is already struggling. Brown rice can also be soaked for several hours before cooking, and then cooked for extra time so it's soft. Tempeh is a fermented soybean product that is easier to digest than soybeans. It has quite a full, savoury taste that makes it popular. Tempeh should not be eaten raw – cook it thoroughly.

rice to make 2 cups when cooked (will vary depending on type of rice chosen)
2 cups peas or sliced green beans
200 g tempeh, sliced
2 tablespoons olive oil
1 clove garlic, minced
1 carrot, diced
2 tablespoons of shoyu
fresh herbs

Boil rice. Steam peas or green beans. Cut tempeh into thin bite-size pieces, stir-fry in a small amount of oil and set aside. Sauté garlic and carrot in oil for three minutes. Add peas or green beans, tempeh and shoyu and mix. Stir-fry for five minutes. Serve with rice and garnish with fresh herbs.

Tuna and celery fried rice

SERVES 4

Tuna is a wonderful food for drying damp in the body. This takes pressure off the spleen and is good if you are trying to lose excess weight or if you have blockages that may cause arthritis. Celery calms aggression and clears heat, which can be very useful in the hot days of summer. The bitter flavour of both celery and corn benefit the heart.

3 cups cooked rice, already cool

2 tablespoons olive oil

black pepper

1 onion, chopped

1 knob ginger, finely chopped

5 stalks celery, chopped

sweet corn from 2 cobs

pinch of salt

425 g canned tuna

2 teaspoons honey (optional)

1 tablespoon sesame oil (optional)

On medium heat, in a heavy-based frying pan, heat one tablespoon of olive oil and add rice and a light sprinkle of freshly ground black pepper. Stir frequently. In a wok, sauté onion and ginger in a tablespoon of oil for two minutes. Add celery and sweet corn. Sprinkle with salt. Reduce heat, cover and allow to steam for 15 minutes. Add tuna and stir through. When tuna is hot, remove from heat. Tip rice from frying pan into wok and stir through. Add honey and stir. Serve in deep bowls and, if desired, drizzle a few drops of sesame oil over each meal.

Stuffed capsicums

Rice is highly nutritious, like wheat, but also has a diuretic effect which stops it being overwhelming and therefore dampening. Peas also support digestion, so this dish is perfect for anyone who is deficient, weak, trying to lose weight or who has a tendency to be cold. This dish is fine for people with excess heat as well.

8 red capsicums, of similar size with flat bottoms
olive oil
2 cups cooked rice
1¹/₂ cups green peas, freshly podded
handful chopped coriander
1 tablespoon freshly chopped mint
fresh herb
tomato juice

Cut tops off all the capsicums so that they can be used later to form a lid. Gently remove seeds, wash and dry. With a brush, oil the outside of the capsicums and place upright in a baking dish. Make sure capsicums are close together for support during cooking. Stuff capsicums with a mixture of rice, peas, coriander and mint. Fill to just over three-quarters full and replace each capsicum's lid. Pour tomato juice into the baking dish so it comes halfway up the capsicums. Add a large sprig of whatever herb looks healthiest in your garden or at the market. Cover dish and cook for an hour and fifteen minutes. Take off lid after an hour so the tops remain crisp. Any leftover filling can be fried until crispy and served on the side with the capsicums.

Zucchini with chervil

Slice and wash baby zucchinis. In a non-stick frying pan or a heavy-based saucepan, combine zucchini with a splash of water and cover. Simmer until tender – zucchini will soon release its own juice. When almost done, add a little butter, chopped chervil and freshly ground black pepper. Serve with SOBA NOODLES.

Soba noodles

Made from buckwheat flour, soba noodles strengthen the digestive system and improve circulation and warmth of the hands and feet. While this might sound a strange benefit in summer, summer naturally supports circulation, so summer is the best time to fix circulation problems.

Fill a large saucepan to the three-quarter mark with water. Add salt and bring to a rolling boil. Add noodles, bring back to boil. Add one cup of cold water. Bring back to boil and add another cup of cold water. Then lower heat and simmer until done. 'Done' will depend on the noodle – to check, remove a noodle and break. If colour and consistency are even inside and out, the noodles are done. Rinse briefly under cold water to stop them sticking together. Serve with shoyu.

Tabouli

Cracked wheat makes a change from consuming wheat in the form of bread or pasta. Wheat benefits the heart, spleen and kidneys and calms the spirit. These can all be sensitive in summer, so wheat is a nutritious and important part of the diet for many people. Tomatoes and cucumber are cooling in the heat of summer and the herbs ensure the dish doesn't become dampening and damage the spleen.

1¹/₂ cups cracked wheat

3 tomatoes, diced

1 small cucumber, finely chopped

handful chives, finely chopped

2 handfuls Italian parsley, chopped

2 handfuls mint leaves, chopped

juice of 1 juicy lemon

1 tablespoon olive oil

freshly ground black pepper

Soak cracked wheat in cold water for ten minutes. Drain and press to remove excess water. Mix cracked wheat with all other ingredients and serve immediately. This is an excellent accompaniment to roast lamb.

Spicy mint yoghurt

Yoghurt is cooling and, especially when combined with lemon juice and pungent herbs, is very nutritious and good for digestion without causing dampness in the body.

1 cup chopped coriander leaves

1 cup chopped mint leaves

1 fresh red chilli (optional)

4 tablespoons lemon juice

250 ml thick yoghurt

In a blender, combine all ingredients except the yoghurt. Add a dash of water and blend. Beat the yoghurt and slowly stir in to blended ingredients.

Poached cherries

SERVES **4**

Cherries build energy and blood and aid digestion. Although the hair predominantly shows the health of the kidneys, its appearance is also affected by the blood. So this dish may improve the appearance of your hair. If it was a windy spring or there have been summer wind storms, cherries may help bring you back into balance, preventing symptoms such as sore throats and dizziness. The lemon juice will add to the cherry's affect on a sore throat and will clear phlegm as well.

500 g cherries, washed, stems and stones removed

1 tablespoon raw sugar

juice of 2 lemons

Put ingredients into a saucepan and cover. Simmer gently for ten minutes. Remove cherries, leaving juice to boil for another two minutes. To serve, pour juice over cherries.

Blue pudding

Blueberries, like other berries, are wonderful summer fare. They nurture kidney yin, and, as the kidney yin provides water to the heart, this is particularly beneficial in summer. The kidney yin helps maintain a calm and grounded outlook on life.

1 large punnet blueberries

3 cups apple juice

1 cup couscous

1 teaspoon grated lemon rind

pinch of salt

Keep a selection of berries aside. Mix all ingredients together in a saucepan. Cover and simmer for ten minutes. Turn off heat and leave undisturbed for 20 minutes. Serve with a few fresh berries on top.

Sweet adzuki dessert

This is an excellent dessert for people trying to remove excess damp and wean tastebuds off desserts big on chocolate and cream.

90 g adzuki beans, pre-soaked

10 lychees

1 piece of mandarin skin

1 tablespoon rock sugar

Amply cover all ingredients with water and bring to the boil. Reduce heat, cover and simmer for 1^1/$_2$ hours. Serve.

CHAPTER SIX

Autumn and its recipes

Traditionally, autumn is the harvest season. Internally, harvesting or gathering energy for the colder months ahead is what our bodies do as well, bringing energy in and moving it down. During autumn, yang, which was dominant in the summer, subsides and the yin grows. There is less activity in the colder months, but more emphasis on substance, on nurturing, supporting and building our organs, fluids and blood, which are the foundations of everything we are and do. After summer, autumn is the time to clear excess heat from the body and then, as temperatures drop, it is time to start warming the body against the extremes of the environment. While this may seem contradictory, summer heat saps strength, while internal warmth supports strength – aim for balance in tune with the changing seasons.

With the arrival of the strong drying winds, many deciduous trees lose their leaves in autumn. The violent winds and dropping temperatures push energy downwards in people in much the same way as it does to many types of trees. While we feel the effects of wind on our skin, internally, the wind attacks the lungs. As the season continues, it often becomes more difficult to breathe in the wind. It is almost as if the wind snatches the oxygen before we breathe in and then blow-dries the little moisture we have left in our airways after the heat of summer. Unless we look after our lungs, autumn can be a time of less oxygen and lowered ability to make the most of the oxygen we do get. Heat and dryness caught in the lungs can cause coughs and lung heat.

According to TCM, wind is a major cause of disease because, while it causes plenty of problems by itself, it can cause dryness and also lead other pathogens into the body such as heat or cold. With all the external wind in autumn, any internal blockages within the body create internal wind that disturbs the liver and exacerbates emotional excess. Although much of the focus in autumn belongs to the lungs, don't forget the liver and gallbladder.

The function of the stomach and intestines often becomes deficient in autumn. Gastro-intestinal diseases are common at this time so that we need to take particular care and eat well to prevent disease finding its way in via the mouth. Without extra care, the body is often poorly equipped to defend itself against excessive wind in autumn.

Dryness

Dryness in the body is most common during autumn and is most likely to affect the lungs and large intestine. Dry lips are a sign of internal dryness. Other symptoms that may indicate internal dryness include dry skin, itchiness, wrinkles, a dry throat, a dry cough and constipation. While more likely to occur with the appropriate seasonal conditions, dryness can show up at any time, depending on your body type and diet.

To treat dryness in autumn, you'll need to add moistening foods to your diet: tofu, tempeh, soy milk, spinach, barley, pears, apples, millet, persimmons, loquat, seaweed, mushrooms, almonds, pine nuts, peanuts, sesame seeds, milk, eggs, clams, crab or pork. Dairy is very nutritious for anyone dry, thin and weak, although it's important only to consume dairy in small amounts so it doesn't create damp and mucus in the body.

Dryness is most likely to affect the zang–fu pair of the lungs and large intestine. If a cough is harsh and dry and accompanied by an extremely dry throat, the lungs need to be cooled to relieve the cough. In this case, cooling foods such as cooked apples and pears, duck, flake, persimmon, celery, nori (a type of seaweed) and octopus may be useful.

For a cough that hangs around for an extended time, a weak, dry cough, a slightly sore throat, night sweats, thirst or symptoms that get worse at night, the lung yin needs supporting. To nourish and moisten the yin of the lung, try pears with apple sauce, dairy products, mutton, tangerines, pine nuts, clams, chicken broth, yams or eggs. As long as there is no sputum, you can also try a little honey in warm water to soothe the throat. If there is phlegm, you can have the honey – raw honey is preferable.

Dry constipation needs a treatment that moistens and lubricates the intestines to help get things moving. There are several foods that fit the bill in autumn including apples, bananas, clams, cheese, honey, milk, peaches, peanut oil, pears, pine nuts, sesame oil or walnuts.

The organs of autumn

Expansiveness and dispersing qualities are associated with the lungs. When the lungs are working well, they expand to take in and hold the air we breathe and then send oxygen all around the body. Lung qi gathers and maintains strength. Lungs that are strong make a person effective in how they go about their tasks and help them to maintain purpose. The large

If your immunity is weak, cut down on salt. Wei qi (the body's protective qi) has an upward energy and salt's downward energy can overwhelm the yang of immunity.

•

Sweating is one way to release anger. Since wei qi controls our ability to sweat, strong lungs can offset an excessive liver. Exercise is beneficial.

•

Honey in warm water before bed will ease a dry throat and a dry cough and assist with dry constipation.

•

The health of the body is important, not just for its own sake, but because of the interconnectedness of the body with the mind and the spirit. Anything done to the body has equal consequence for the mind and spirit also. If you feel good physically, you will be more balanced emotionally, mentally and spiritually.

•

Anger means the qi is rocking inside the body, rather than floating and happy.

intestine, or colon (the lungs' fu partner) lets go of what is no longer necessary. If there is a healthy balance between the lungs and the colon, a person will be able to honour commitments, but let go when a relationship is over. This balance promotes the ability to experience and then let go of sadness, and to keep track of possessions without becoming overly attached to them.

The strength of the lungs dictates how effective the lungs are at looking after our immune systems. The lungs mix qi from food essence sent up by the spleen and qi from the air to form our defence system – the body's protective qi, called wei qi. Wei qi is a yang form of energy and is warm and aggressive. It protects the skin, nose and mouth (and therefore the lungs) from external attack by viruses, colds and germs. These external attacks are often led by wind.

At its strongest, wei qi protects us against all attacks from the weather and disease-causing elements that may attempt to infiltrate the body from the environment. During the day, wei qi circulates near the skin, ready to defend us against germs, opening and closing pores to allow us to sweat. It is closest to our skin at noon each day, so our immunity is strongest at this time. At night, it moves to the inner core and into our internal organs – it is important to dress warmly when we go out at night because our bodies' protective qi assumes we are in a safe, warm place at night, rather than out on the town.

While wei qi is controlled by the lungs, it is created by the spleen working with the kidneys. If wei qi isn't working well, you'll get every cold and virus that is 'going around'. If you are already sick, then you need to treat your cold or illness, however when you are well, you can strengthen the yang of your digestive system and kidneys to strengthen wei qi. An important part of building wei qi is to avoid too much sweating, which allows qi to disperse. Diet can play a part in this. Fresh ginger is warm and encourages sweating, whereas dry ginger is warming but doesn't induce sweating. If your wei qi is weak, try eating fresh ginger when you are sick, to let the illness escape from the body and dry ginger between colds, to build the wei qi. If you are getting sick regularly, avoid very spicy foods because they are likely to encourage the body to sweat. Astragalus (huang qi) mixed with dang-shen in broth may also be helpful to build wei qi between colds.

The emotion of grief is housed in the lungs. If grief is repressed, it festers in the body and, over time, causes the lungs to contract, which means the lungs can't extract sufficient qi from the air or distribute that qi around the body. The undistributed qi slowly clogs up the lungs. And wei qi, and our ability to fend off pathogens, weakens. If grief continues, it can lead to detachment and vulnerability and can manifest physically as asthma or chronic coughing unrelated to a cold. Some health issues with the large intestines may also be connected with unresolved grief. Along with deep breathing, meditation, counselling and exercise, pungent foods may help clear grief by balancing the lung qi.

The lungs' connection with the skin and wei qi means that the skin reflects the condition of the lungs and, particularly during autumn, that it needs to be strong enough to keep wind out. In autumn, we can increase the amount of oil we eat to give the skin more protection. If the lungs are strong, skin will be lustrous and firm.

The pungent flavour

Food and herbs with a pungent flavour are important for the lungs. Pungents are yang and ascending, which means they move up into the lungs to open and clear them. While pungents are useful to promote the lungs at any time of the year, this is particularly important when the lungs are at their most sensitive during autumn. Pungents are excellent for clearing wind from the body too as they encourage movement and flow. Pungents encouraging wind to leave the body may also remove other potential disease-causers with the wind. Examples of pungent foods are bay leaves, capers, caraway seeds, cardamom, chives, cinnamon, cloves, cumquats, dill, fennel, leek, oregano, nutmeg, rosemary, safflower, taro, thyme, turmeric, watercress, wheat germ, cabbage, turnip, ginger, horse-radish, pepper, onions, garlic and chillies.

The expansive nature of pungent herbs means that, while they are important to strengthen the lungs, they shouldn't be overused in autumn, as it is a yin and contracting time. Sour foods should also be included in the diet to help protect the skin against attack from the wind.

Heat and phlegm in the lungs

Heat in the lungs is common in autumn, because of the combining factors of the remaining heat of summer and the windy, drying effects of early autumn. The symptoms can include fevers with chills, red tongue with yellow coating, dry cough, shortness of breath, sore throat and yellow nasal discharge. If this is how you're feeling, you'll need foods to cool the heat and clear the mucus. Cooked apples and pears, peaches, citrus fruits, persimmons, seaweed, mushrooms, daikon radishes, watercress, carrots, radishes, pumpkin, cabbage, bok choy, cauliflower, chard or papayas should help to cool and clear the lungs.

If you have heat signs in autumn, such as a red face or a red tongue with a yellow coat, try congee of millet, barley or rice with watercress. Avoid warming foods such as beef, lamb, chicken (especially fried), cinnamon, fennel, ginger (except in small amounts) and especially coffee, onions and garlic. Always choose foods based on the season. If you have these symptoms in winter, use pumpkin, cabbage and bok choy.

When you have a cold or flu and develop lung phlegm, it can be heard in a rattling cough or seen when you cough up thick sputum. To know whether the phlegm comes from the lungs rather than the stomach, look for sticky phlegm, wheezing, asthma, a white or yellow greasy tongue coat and shortness of breath. Stomach phlegm is usually a result of poor digestion.

Pungent flavours can be used to clear mucus from the lungs – if heat signs are present, make sure you use cooling pungents such as peppermint or chamomile. For hot phlegm (hot phlegm is yellow or green), use cooling damp removers such as watercress, radish, daikon radish, and seaweed. For cold phlegm (white), use warming damp removers such as fennel, cayenne, garlic, onions, mustard greens, horseradish and ginger. Several foods can be used to clear either hot or cold phlegm in the lungs, including potato, pumpkin,

Mushrooms, carrots and figs are all good for reducing excesses such as a red face, extreme emotions and a loud voice.

•

When building deficiency, it is important to go gently, so as not to go to the other extreme. In TCM, this is referred to as protecting the righteous qi, so that you get rid of the problem without causing any damage. So if you've been sick, build yourself up slowly with warming soups.

•

Consider your genetic inheritance when you eat. If your parents and grandparents are from a vegetarian culture, you are likely to thrive on a vegetarian diet. If you are a descendent of a meat-eating culture, you will benefit from some animal products, even if you choose a predominantly vegetarian diet.

•

For a sore throat, tonsillitis or dog bite, peel a potato. Juice it, and apply externally to the throat or the bite wound.

During autumn, avoid cold drinks and raw or cold food.

•

Leek congee is gently warming, and will be helpful for anyone suffering from chronic diarrhoea.

•

In autumn, pine nut congee can be useful for constipation. It is especially good if taken for breakfast. The rice is gentle on the digestive system, and also calming for the mind, while the pine nuts moisten and balance the large intestine and cause a sliding effect.

•

If wind rises to the head, it causes dizziness. Strokes can sometimes be the long-term outcome of anger-causing yang rising to the head.

•

Having something to eat or drink when you're angry can be very calming because, when the mouth is chewing, the mind tends to let go of the anger and concentrate on the food – but calm down substantially first.

linseed, turnip, Job's tears barley, tuna and mushrooms. If you have a persistent cough or asthma, see your health practitioner.

Deficient lung yin and blood

Weak lung yin can occur after a chronic infection that has run the body down, and any yin deficiency in the lungs means the kidney yin is also likely to need a boost. A dry cough that rarely produces sputum, occasional fever, frequent thirst, red cheeks and tongue, night sweats and hot palms and soles all indicate a yin deficiency. Eat foods that strengthen yin, especially the yin of the lungs and kidneys and use cooking methods such as steaming and boiling. Seaweed, oranges, pears, peaches, watermelon, soy products, green beans, pork, dairy products, eggs, oysters and clams are all autumn yin-builders. Include foods that are easy on the digestive system. Try a couple of figs. In autumn, foods that nourish the blood include figs, pears and pumpkin. Root vegetables such as parsnip, potato and beetroot can help nourish the blood for the cooler weather.

Weak lung qi and immunity

Lung qi flows downwards. When lung qi is weak, the lungs don't draw in as much air from the environment and then they are unable to push oxygen strongly throughout the body. This affects how energetic we feel. The other consequence of a weak lung qi is that it doesn't apply the appropriate force on the large intestine to assist with pushing waste out. The result can be constipation, because the colon isn't encouraged to let go.

Most lung problems show up as a cough or shortness of breath. If you've been getting colds and flu a lot, a good tonic to boost immunity is leek soup, as it strengthens both lung yang and wei qi. You can also try making a broth out of white onions and unrefined brown sugar. Make sure the broth isn't too salty as salt pushes energy down, whereas wei qi is an upward-moving energy. Remember, these are options when you are well, not after you've already got a cold. If you try to strengthen wei qi while you have a cold, it locks the body, trapping the cold and making recovery much more difficult. To fight off a cold successfully, you need to take action on the first day. Use the spring onion and sweat technique (see page 41). Otherwise you'll just have to rest up and be gentle on yourself so the cold runs its course without complications.

Avoiding damp in the dry season

Since the spleen and stomach may be weak in autumn, it is necessary to eat foods to ease the digestion process. As in every season, when the spleen is unable to cope with its work-load, the result is damp. This is an excess of damp caused by a deficiency in the spleen. Well-cooked, warm foods with vegetables and plenty of grains, such as rice, are the best foods to nurture the spleen. Dampness within the spleen can cause a thick and greasy tongue coat, feelings of heaviness, poor appetite, abdominal distension and watery stools. In autumn, drain damp with mushrooms. Other foods that clear damp from the lungs in autumn are the same as those that clear phlegm from the lungs.

Dampness can affect the joints, as arthritis, or the body's energy pathways, which can cause slow or difficult movement or numbness. Arthritis, rheumatism and tennis elbow may be caused by dampness

Bok choy and liver: wash and chop bok choy. Fry in wok with oil, ginger and salt. Then add a little hot water. When it's steaming, add liver, brown and serve. Add tofu before the liver if you have excessive heat in the body.

•

Persimmon skins can be used in soup to stop diarrhoea.

•

Pumpkin seeds act as a sedative on worms so that the worms release the hold that is keeping them inside you. Either use a mortar and pestle or chew the pumpkin seeds very well so their sharp ends don't damage the stomach lining. Follow the seeds with bran to flush the large intestine, and the worms will end up in the toilet bowl.

•

Seaweed helps clear goitre – try it in soup.

blocking the energy paths in the body. These energy paths are known as meridians. Symptoms of damp-related meridian blockages are often aggravated by dampness in the weather. Foods that help open the meridians and clear blockages include black sesame, black soybeans, capers, dried ginger, Job's tears barley, turnips, mulberries and pine nuts.

Green tea can help remove damp from the body through urination – which is why many Chinese people sip green tea when they eat very fatty, damp-causing, meals. This way they get the nutrition from the food without also getting the dampness. But don't gulp during meals as too much liquid will flood the spleen and cause more damp.

If you often have a runny nose or a cold, have eaten dairy products excessively for most of your life, have lung problems (such as asthma) or colon problems and a thick coating on the tongue, you will most likely benefit from the following tea to remove damp – especially in autumn. To half a litre of water, add a pinch of fennel seeds, fenugreek seeds (if you have any heat signs use less fenugreek), linseed (if the brew is too sticky use less linseed), nettle leaf and liquorice root. Simmer for 45 minutes in a covered pot, strain and allow to cool sufficiently to drink.

Dampness in the body often clouds your enthusiasm, especially in the early stages of changing the way you eat, and look at food. This can make it difficult to remember why you are bothering. Because of their clearing ability, pungent foods can quickly help people who are lacking in energy and motivation. Of course, adding a few pungent foods won't fix everything, but they might make you feel light enough to enjoy the process of eating well. Something else to consider is that warm pungents, such as onions and garlic, can increase appetite. So if you have a tendency to overeat, choose cooler pungents.

How the organs work together in autumn

The kidneys play an important role in the health of the lungs, so looking after the kidneys should be part of a balanced diet in autumn. The kidney qi, which is upward-moving, reaches up within the body and grabs onto the downward moving lung qi, helping the lung qi by pulling it down. If you find your breath feels shallow, try eating to support the kidneys as well as the lungs. In autumn, that includes fennel, fenugreek, walnuts, millet, black beans, sardines, lamb and salmon.

Good health in autumn sets us up for good health in winter and spring. This is especially so with the liver. Problems with the liver are difficult to live with. For example, stagnant liver qi can lead to depression, pre-menstrual tension, irritability, impatience, confusion and resistance to change. The physical symptoms can include distension, burping, sighing, tiredness or irregular periods. The liver can be too sensitive in spring to strengthen it then, however autumn can be the perfect time and then the liver will cope better in spring. So eat plenty of spinach.

Several autumn foods benefit the liver. Dill calms the liver, plums and leeks remove stagnation and chestnuts improve blood circulation and may ease menstrual clotting. Hypertension, which affects the heart, but usually comes from the liver, may be reduced in autumn with persimmons.

There are other flow-on effects for the health between seasons. For instance, diarrhoea (caused by a spleen/stomach weakness) in the late summer can lead to bronchitis (caused by lung weakness) in the autumn. This is because nutrition that should have gone to build and support the lungs and create wei qi was lost due to the diarrhoea.

So, what to eat in autumn?

Look on the seasonal charts – autumn is a wonderful season for apprecia-tors of food. After the long, warm growing season provided by spring and summer, the benefits are there to be reaped. Autumn food should mois-ten and clear the lungs, get rid of wind, and support the digestive system.

Start with foods that moisten the lungs, such as apples and pears, although people with damp should use fruit and all moistening foods sparingly. Apples, persimmons and pears contain a lot of water, so are very good for getting rid of fire in the heart and stomach that may be left over from summer. Lima beans and navy beans are good for the lungs. Use pungent foods and herbs to stimulate and clear the lungs. Try spearmint. If you have heat in the lungs, you'll need to choose cooling pungents such as peppermint.

Since the digestive system is often deficient in autumn, it is important to adjust what you eat as soon as autumn arrives. Although it might still be hot on some days, it is important to avoid excessive intake of cold drinks and summer fruits such as melons. Otherwise, there is a risk of damage to the stomach and spleen. Eat dark green and orange vegetables to assist digestion. Figs are great for strengthening the stomach and the spleen too. Sour and sweet foods for autumn include adzuki beans, apples, cheese, grapes, olives and sourdough bread. These support the spleen, while encouraging energy downwards. As the spleen and stomach can be deficient in autumn, foods that harmonise the middle burner are very useful. Try millet, chestnuts, rice and carrots.

Warm foods protect the liver and the whole body against the symptoms of wind because they encourage movement and leave no opening for wind. Cold food, on the other hand, slows the digestive process and encourages wind. If you have flatulence, eat more cooked vegetables with some pungents to encourage the bowel to loosen and expel the wind.

Sometimes cold foods damage the digestion process and cause diarrhoea. In this case, you'll need to follow a gentle diet of cooked vegetables until the symptoms pass. Sweet foods also encourage wind in the body. Sinking foods, such as most seafood, push wind down and out.

In autumn, there should be far fewer salads and more soups. Soups are good in autumn for several reasons, including the longer cooking times that mean the ingredients are easier to digest, and the watery medium that nurtures yin. Change the way food is prepared too.

Autumn is a good time for steaming, which supports yin. Cook at low temperatures for longer periods of time than you would for a quick stir-fry in summer. Heavy foods, such as thick stews and soups build energy reserves for the colder months. Salt helps to moisten dryness and sends energy downwards, so use small amounts of salt in cooking – add a splash of shoyu or use a little seaweed.

Wheat can be damp-causing in people who already have a substantial problem. In contrast, rye dries damp. Try eating rye bread – toast it for that extra drying effect. Sourdough rye benefits the liver, because of its sour flavour, as well as removing damp.

•

During autumn, use tahini as a flavouring in soups and stews or as a spread for toast or sandwiches. Tahini is gentler on the digestive system than unprocessed sesame seeds, but still provides the benefits of building the yin and toning all the major organs, but particularly the liver and kidneys.

•

In the past, meat eaters tended to eat a wider variety or parts of an animal including the intestines, tongue, bone marrow, blood and organs such as brains, kidneys and liver. This balance can also be achieved by eating smaller fish or animals such as anchovies, sardines, snails or oysters.

Horseradish, white pepper, onions, garlic and chillies are examples of pungent foods that should be used sparingly as they are quite strong. Sage, raw onion and hot peppers (all very pungent) are too extreme for people with imbalances of wind or dryness, which can be prevalent in autumn. Most of us fare better when most of our pungency comes from gentler sources. Thin, nervous or weak people and people with heat should always stick to gentler pungents. Try basil and coriander (early in the season), bay leaves, cabbage, capers, caraway seed, cardamom, chives, cinnamon, cloves, cumquat, dill, fennel, ginger, leek, oregano, nutmeg, rosemary, safflower, taro, thyme, turmeric, turnip, watercress and wheat germ.

Energy moves down in autumn, so as the season progresses, we can eat more foods that have downward moving energy, such as root vegetables. Seaweed, which is sinking, can be used to clear thick mucus without causing drying. Bitter foods help by bringing energy into the lower body too. Bitter strengthens the kidneys and lungs, and as bitter also drains damp and is cooling, bitter foods are especially good for clearing up yellow phlegm in the lungs. Examples of foods that are bitter and pungent include citrus peel, radish leaf, scallion, turnip and white pepper.

Astringent and sour foods encourage contraction, which fits in with the seasonal direction and stimulates the liver. In the liver, sour helps breakdown grease and fats. Sour strengthens lungs and 'grounds' the heart. Sour foods, such as the sour and pungent leek, are appropriate for autumn which can be seen as a time of contraction. Other examples include sourdough bread, sauerkraut, olives, pickles, adzuki beans, umebosi plums, rose hip tea, vinegar, yoghurt, lemons, limes, grapefruit, and sour plums and apples.

Later in autumn, cabbage supports the liver qi and relaxes the intestines, so it works with the other ingredients to get rid of constipation without causing diarrhoea. Interestingly, the ancient Greeks thought cabbage could both prevent drunkenness and cure a hangover – which in TCM terms are both related to the liver. Since it is always important to calm and support the liver, nature has provided several liver supporters for autumn. To remove liver stagnancy that is causing general frustration or blood clotting during menstruation, try mustard greens, chestnuts, pine nuts, turmeric, cumin or ginger. Use sour foods such as salted plums (umebosi plums) or lime to reduce liver excess.

If you feel angry or have a poor appetite, it may be because the liver is heated. To cool and detoxify the liver use plums, mushrooms or millet. Lamb, pork or beef liver congee is an excellent way to rejuvenate your own neglected or abused liver. Chicken liver may also be used but only if you have no signs of heat. Foods to reduce liver wind symptoms in autumn include celery and pine nuts.

Pork is the most moistening meat and is very nutritious, so it's perfect to eat in autumn. After the yang of summer, pork enriches the yin, which in turn strengthens both blood production and flow. Figs provide moisture to areas that tend to dry out in autumn such as the throat. In fact, all sweet-flavoured foods moisten dryness to some degree. In autumn, plums also build yin and blood.

Tempeh, like mushrooms, works well with meat flavours. And the meat tends to balance the cooling properties of the tempeh. Try tempeh fried with mild European sausages and mixed with stir-fried vegetables. In autumn and spring, it can be cooked with ginger or other herbs to clear wind and damp.

Bok choy is helpful when the body is run-down, or when the body feels warm enough but the hands and feet are cold. Improving circulation in early autumn will be much easier than living with the consequences in the depths of winter. If the tongue is showing cold signs (if it is pale or has a white coating), or you're feeling very cold on the torso, make sure you add ginger, garlic or meat to any meal with bok choy.

Autumn is the season for most nuts. As nuts can go rancid very easily, it is important to buy only nuts still in their shells; however, in autumn, you shouldn't have any trouble getting fresh nuts. Especially in the cooler months, cooked (usually roasted) nuts and seeds are easier to digest. Nuts and seeds are a concentrated food source. They are best for people who are weak or thin. If you are overweight or have signs of heat, such as a red tongue or face, limit the number of nuts you eat.

Autumn recipes

Beef congee

SERVES 1

Beef is sweet and warm. People who are tired with loose bowels, losing weight, are low on energy or are feeling run-down can eat beef as a pick-me-up. Try a beef congee. This will tonify the blood and should provide an energy boost. You can eat beef congee in any season, but not on a hot day. (See pages 124–125 for suggestions of other ingredients to include in a congee.)

100 g beef, chopped very finely

1-2 slices ginger, finely chopped

dash tamari (or any naturally brewed soy sauce)

150 g rice

Combine beef, ginger and tamari in a bowl and set aside to marinate. Choose a heavy-based saucepan. Add rice and water. Use four parts water to one part rice. Bring to a boil and then cover and simmer for approximately 45 minutes or until rice is soft and flaky. Add the beef, ginger and tamari marinade. Bring back to a boil and simmer for a further ten minutes until the beef is cooked. The congee can then be served or it can be simmered (covered) for a further two to three hours. Maintain enough water to keep a soupy consistency during cooking. Serve in small bowls.

Chicken tonic

Chicken tonic strengthens the digestion system, the liver (which tonifies the eyes and may ease blurring of vision), the kidneys (which eases lower back pain) and improves blood circulation and counteracts anaemia, dizziness, fatigue and greying hair. This dish is also good for people who have undergone chemotherapy or older people who are feeling weak and constipated.

There are two other important things to know about this dish: it can make diarrhoea worse; and onion or garlic should never be added to CHICKEN TONIC because they can react with the fleeceflower root.

1 chicken fillet, chopped into bite-sized pieces

15 g fleeceflower root (he shou wu)

15 g Chinese angelica root (dang gui)

15 g wolfberry fruit (gou qi zi)

Boil 700 ml of water and add all ingredients. Cover and simmer for two hours. Serve chicken with steamed rice and drink the liquid. Add shoyu for taste.

Bean and turnip soup

SERVE 6

Soup naturally supports yin qualities. It is calming and nurturing, and is particularly balancing for people who eat meat, oil and plenty of other yang foods. Longer cooking times generate more heat and so increase a meal's warming qualities, which is particularly good to keep the cold at bay. Wakame, a type of seaweed, builds yin, counteracts dryness and removes phlegm. It may also improve the appearance of the hair. Lima beans are good for the lungs and yin and the appearance of the skin. Turnips improve circulation and build blood, which also affects the appearance of the hair. It's tempting to call this 'hair and skin soup'.

12 cm wakame, broken into pieces and soaked

1 cup soaked lima beans

$^1/_2$ onion, finely chopped

2 carrots, cut into fat half moons

4 turnips, cut in similar size to carrots

1 cup cabbage, shredded

1 tablespoon miso

With wakame and beans, bring six cups of water to the boil. Reduce heat, cover and simmer for $1^1/_2$ hours. Add vegetables and simmer further 40 minutes. Beans and vegetables should be soft. Add miso and simmer five more minutes. Serve with sourdough bread.

Qi soup

This simple broth needs a long cooking time to really let the ingredients blend properly, however, it is worth the wait as it should improve digestion, and increase qi and strength.

1 litre lamb stock

corn from 3 cobs

4 potatoes, cubed

3 silverbeet leaves, finely shredded

1 knob ginger

Add all ingredients to a heavy-based saucepan and simmer covered for three hours. Add a little salt and serve.

Leek and potato soup

SERVES 4

This soup builds energy, improves digestion and strengthens the liver, lungs and kidneys. Both its texture and ingredients help people who have problems swallowing. It is warming, calming and comforting. It may also ease diarrhoea and rheumatism.

3 leeks, sliced

1 teaspoon butter

1 litre chicken stock

4 potatoes, cubed

1 sweet potato, cubed

freshly ground pepper

handful fresh parsley

yoghurt

In a large saucepan with a heavy base, sauté leeks in butter on low heat until they are soft and clear. Add stock and potatoes (including the sweet potato). Cover and simmer for three quarters of an hour. Add pepper and parsley. Blend and serve with a dollop of natural yoghurt and extra parsley.

Pork and bok choy soup

SERVES 4

Pork builds yin and moistens dryness. Bok choy is great for anyone who is run down or if circulation to the hands and feet is poor. Mandarin peel, which you can buy from a Chinese grocery, supports the spleen and pushes rebellious stomach qi down, which may be causing burping. Almonds moisten the lungs, to ease coughs, and the large intestine, to ease constipation.

1 teaspoon olive oil

1 small onion, finely chopped

300 g pork meat with fat removed, cut into bite-sized pieces

$^1/_2$ teaspoon salt

bunch bok choy, washed and coarsely chopped

handful dried tangerine peel

15 Chinese almonds

Heat oil in the bottom of a large saucepan and add onion. Sauté onions until soft, then remove. Place pork and salt in a pot with $1^1/_2$ litres of water and heat to a rolling boil. Re-add onions and all other ingredients except a couple of pieces of bok choy. Cover and simmer for two hours, adding the last of the bok choy a minute or two before removing the saucepan from the heat. Serve warm.

Mustard greens with crab sauce

SERVES 4 AS A SIDE DISH

This dish may help to clear lungs of congestion and coughs with phlegm, and take extra heat out of the liver that may be exacerbating anger.

120 g crab meat, broken up

150 ml milk

$^1/_2$ teaspoon salt

450 g washed mustard greens

2 tablespoons sesame oil

1 teaspoon cornflour

Put crabmeat in a saucepan with milk and salt and cook on moderate heat. Chop the greens. In a wok, sauté greens in oil on high heat for four minutes. Drain and arrange on four plates. Mix cornflour with a few drops of water and then add to the crab and stir until thickened. Pour over greens and serve as a side dish to fried rice.

Figs with chicken

SERVES 6

People with weak yin can experience a dry mouth, constipation or ringing in the ears. As dryness is often prevalent during the autumn, this dish will moisten the body, ease constipation and sooth a dry tongue or throat. Omit the ginger if there are signs of heat.

5 g almonds

1 chicken

8 fresh figs, cut in half

1 handful bamboo shoots

2 pieces ginger

pinch of salt

Soak almonds and rub off skin. Boil chicken in water for five minutes, then discard water, remove flesh from the bones and cut meat into bite-sized pieces. Boil $1^1/_2$ litres water, add all ingredients except salt, cover and simmer for two hours. Add salt and serve with rice.

Pork, pak choy, cabbage and figs

SERVES 2

If you have a dry throat or a dry cough or constipation, this dish will help to moisten the inside of the body and relieve these symptoms. It helps nourish the yin of lungs, spleen and liver as well as the blood.

250 g pork, thinly sliced, with any visible fat removed
8 leaves pak choy cabbage, including leafy top and long white stalk
4 dried figs

Add ingredients to $1^1/_2$ litres of water and bring to the boil. Simmer gently, uncovered, until the water is reduced to approximately half a litre which will take about $1^1/_2$ hours. Add shoyu to taste and serve with rice.

Freshwater fish with papaya

SERVES 2

This dish is excellent for nursing mothers as it builds up the milk supply.
It is also useful for oedema and fluid retention. The papaya can encourage
bowel movement and treats some types of rheumatism.

300 g whole freshwater fish

300 g papaya, skin removed (between firm and ripe is best for this recipe)

Clean and scale fish. Cut fish into two pieces. Cut papaya into two pieces of
similar size to the fish pieces. Place fish and papaya into a saucepan and
cover with water at double the height of the ingredients. Gently simmer until
liquid, which becomes a milky colour, is reduced by half. Remove bones.
Serve in a bowl with rice.

Millet and mushroom bake

Like all the grains, millet is fine for any season. But it is particularly good for autumn as it gets rid of heat (that may be a summer leftover), moistens dryness (the most common autumn problem) and supports yin and the kidneys for the upcoming winter. Mushrooms ease coughs and get rid of phlegm as well as strengthening the lungs. If you have a great deal of phlegm, swap the millet for rice.

3 cups millet
pinch of salt
1 tablespoon olive oil
$^1/_2$ cup flour (unrefined)
$^1/_2$ onion, chopped
200 g mushrooms, sliced
3 tablespoons tamari
parsley

Soak millet in water overnight. Drain. Add millet, fresh water (8 cups) and salt to a pot and bring to a boil. Reduce heat and simmer for 35 minutes.

While you prepare other ingredients, preheat the oven to 180°C. Place millet in an oiled casserole dish. In a frying pan, sauté onions and mushrooms until soft. Then add flour, and stir in with the mushrooms and onions, before adding $1^1/_2$ cups of water. Stirring continuously. Bring almost to the boil, then cover, reduce heat and simmer for five minutes. Add tamari and simmer for a further ten minutes. Pour contents of frying pan into the casserole dish and stir very lightly with the millet. Bake for 20 minutes. Cut into four slices, garnish with parsley and serve with lightly steamed spinach.

Chilli con carne

In this dish, the herbs clear the lungs and digestive system and stop any potential dampness. The beef and beans warm and build yin, while the tomatoes remove heat from the beef and herbs.

500 g borlotti beans, pre-soaked overnight and drained

300 g steak, cut into small cubes

2 onions, chopped

3 bay leaves

2 tablespoons olive oil

500 g tomatoes, peeled and chopped

3 okra, sliced

pinch of salt

2 teaspoons freshly ground black pepper

2 teaspoons paprika

2 teaspoons ground cardamom

$^1/_2$ teaspoon ground cumin

2 tablespoons polenta

Place beans, meat, onion and bay leaves in a heavy-based casserole dish. Just cover with cold water. Warm slowly, then cover and simmer until beans are cooked (check after two hours as you may need to add a little extra water). Heat oven to 180°C. In a heavy frying pan, heat oil, stir in tomatoes, okra, spices and polenta. Simmer for ten minutes, then tip in with the meat and beans. Place casserole dish in the oven and cook for another hour.

Stir-fried prawns with okra

SERVES 4

Breast-feeding mothers or men wanting to father a child may benefit from this dish. It strengthens the liver and kidneys and offers an energy boost for people who have been feeling light-headed or lacking in direction.

1 slice ginger, finely chopped

1 stalk lemon grass, cut in large pieces

1 tablespoon olive oil

8 spring onions, chopped

12 prawns, shelled, with heads and veins removed

12 small okra, finely chopped

2 tablespoons chicken stock

2 tablespoons tamari (or any naturally brewed soy sauce)

2 teaspoons raw honey

Sauté ginger and lemon grass in oil. Add spring onions and stir through with oil and ginger. Add prawns and okra and stir with heat on high. Then add stock, cover and turn heat to medium. Steam for one to two minutes. Remove lemon grass, then stir through tamari and remove from heat. Stir through honey and serve with steamed rice.

Lamb's liver and bacon

Bacon can be fatty, so it's not something you'd want to eat everyday, but it is extremely tasty and, in autumn, it can help strengthen the skin against wind and dryness. This dish is great to strengthen and support our livers and kidneys. It can help us adjust to the cold weather, and it can improve the appearance of hair and eyes. As with any very nutritious food, a little goes a long way.

$^1/_2$ tablespoon olive oil
4 rashers streaky bacon
8 thin slices lamb's liver
1 handful plain flour
freshly ground black pepper
4 tablespoons lamb stock
pinch of salt

In a teaspoon of oil, fry bacon until it is crisp. Remove bacon and keep warm. Make sure liver pieces are skinned and have no flecks of green on them. If there is any green, remove with a knife. Finely coat liver with flour and a twist of freshly ground black pepper. If necessary, add a little oil to the pan. Briefly sauté both sides until the liver is brown. Remove any excess fat from the pan, heat stock, add salt and pour over liver. Serve liver and bacon with a green side vegetable such as steamed bok choy.

Fruit salad

SERVES 4

Dried fruit has been used for centuries to enjoy the benefits of one season within another. The drying process actually changes the nature of foods, sending energy in and making them appropriate for the colder months, which is why it is fine to have dried summer fruits, such as apricots, in May. Many of the ingredients in this fruit salad moisten the lungs, so it is perfect for autumn.

1 stick cinnamon

2 cloves

small handful of each of several dried fruits such as apples, peaches, dates, figs, sultanas and apricots

1 slightly smaller handful of chopped almonds and pecans

1 teaspoon honey

$^1/_2$ teaspoon saffron, ground

1 vanilla bean, split lengthways

3 strips lemon zest

1 orange

Wrap cinnamon and cloves in a fine cloth so the flavour can mix with the other ingredients and so you will be able to remove them from the pot prior to serving. Add wrap and all other ingredients to a saucepan and cover with cold water. Slowly bring to the boil, then simmer for 15 minutes, stirring occasionally. Remove vanilla bean. Garnish with thin wedges of orange and serve.

Orange porridge

SERVES 3-4

This is an excellent source of nourishment for a weak spleen or stomach. If you've had any digestion problems or have been feeling weak or you have had a long illness or if you are a new mother, this is a suitable tonic. It is good for the kidneys and the lungs. Sweet potato strengthens qi, expels cold and tones the stomach and spleen; rice helps the spleen and stomach; lotus seed tones the spleen, heart, kidneys qi and blood; and longan can be used to treat weakness.

500 g sweet potato, thinly sliced

1 cup white rice

¹/₄ cup lotus seeds

1 carrot, thinly sliced

¹/₄ cup Job's tears barley

4 dried longans, chopped

dash of sesame oil

dash of honey

pinch of salt

Combine all ingredients, except the oil, honey and salt, in a slow cooker or a crockpot. Mix and cover to double their height with water. Cover and simmer for four to five hours. Check water level after three hours. Add salt, honey and oil to taste and serve warm.

CHAPTER SEVEN

Winter and its recipes

Winter is the season of hibernation – when energy moves inward. A time when stillness and quiet seem to amplify what sound there is. Yin qi is highlighted and yang qi is subdued. Winter foods such as grains, dried or preserved food, seeds and nuts have an inward-moving energy too. In winter, meals should be nutritious and warming. And it's a time of gentle celebration where food and family connection is promoted. In winter, it's appropriate to drink a small amount of spirits or wine to warm the system up, since they are hot-warm in nature, promote circulation, stimulate the appetite, relieve tiredness and keep out the cold.

In Australia, because of our relatively temperate climate you might be tempted to pretend winter doesn't exist. But don't let this opportunity pass you by. Respond to the season by rugging up and eating delicious stews and soups.

Enjoy the chance to revel in your own company and that of close friends and family with cosy gatherings and plenty of warming, comforting foods. Many cultures have the majority of their celebrations that involve food in winter, whereas because northern hemisphere cultures have been transplanted here, most Australians feast in the warmer months. New traditions can be created – cook up a warming feast in winter and invite people you love over.

Cold

The cold that surrounds us in winter can easily seep into our bodies. Cold causes contraction, so movement becomes limited, which makes us even colder. If you are suffering from internal cold, it can show up as poor circulation, aches and pains, asthma, arthritis or colitis.

Turtle beans are yin-building and the most warming legume, but others, such as adzuki beans (as long as you are not dry internally) and lentils, can be made more warming by adding a warming herb such as rosemary. Pine nuts, anchovies, mussels, trout, walnuts and chestnuts are also warming. If you have cold damp, you can encourage circulation with warming herbs such as ginger, cloves, fennel and anise.

There can be many reasons for abdominal pain. This can complicate things if you're trying to work out the problem at home. The best thing you can do is to use the tools you already have – knowledge of your basic symptoms and how your tongue looks – then see if you can effect a change in how you feel with a change in your diet. If pain persists, see a health professional.

That said, one of the most common causes of pain in the abdomen in winter is from cold. Sometimes it's possible to feel the cold externally. Place your hand on the stomach, all around the region that is hurting. Does the skin feel cold? Another common cause of abdominal pain is weakness in the stomach and spleen. These pains often get worse when you are tired or hungry. Fortunately, there are dishes that may ease both of these conditions at once. Try a leek and potato soup – consider adding lamb.

Aspirin and Vitamin C tablets are both cold causing. In winter, you might want to try an alternative to aspirin for pain and get your Vitamin C from food sources such as pumpkin soup or a warm fruit compote.

Cold within the body restricts blood flow. If you experience pain, especially in the lower back or in the tummy, less blood flow makes the pain worse. Pain during periods is often caused by cold or lack of qi movement within the body. During menstruation, the body is very open to allow the bleeding, however that same openness makes the body susceptible to cold. The best foods for a woman experiencing a painful period are warm in both temperature and nature.

Another possible cause for painful periods is stagnant liver qi or poor blood circulation caused by eating too much salt. The lack of movement caused by stagnation leads to the same effect (cold) and is helped by the same warm diet.

In winter, get rid of phlegm with kohlrabi. For a dry cough, use seaweed.

•

At the onset of the common cold, try fresh ginger boiled in water with the white parts of two spring onion stalks. Boil for ten minutes to make a warming broth to give you energy (without strengthening the cold) and to dispel cold and wind.

•

A cold with a runny nose may be treated with lemon in warm water because the lemon is astringent (which should ease the runny nose) and warm. If your nose and sinuses are blocked and your tongue is pale, try cinnamon and honey, as the cinnamon will warm you and the honey should loosen the blockage.

•

The common cold is often caused by an invasion of cold wind. Cold wind usually enters the body when you get cold. Prime targets are exposed necks and lower backs.

The ability to listen clearly is sharpest during winter. This doesn't mean only listening to conversations, but listening to your own body and comprehending its needs, as well as having a deeper understanding of yourself and your interactions with others.

•

The rise and fall of a baby's tummy as it breathes shows a strong kidney yang pulling the breath into the body.

•

Foods that strengthen the kidneys benefit the ears and hearing.

•

Pork kidney is often used in the treatment of old-age deafness.

•

A little salt is good. But more salt is not necessarily better. Salt slows the circulation of the blood, which is bad for people with heart problems or high blood pressure, and increases fluid retention and appetite, which makes it hard to shed extra weight.

The organs of winter

The kidneys and bladder are the yin–yang, zang–fu pair associated with winter, and both are sensitive to the cold. While other seasons and organs demand a balance, it is almost impossible to be too good to the kidneys – they are considered the gate of life and store our very essence. Our longevity is directly related to the health of the kidneys. Supporting them becomes increasingly important as we get older.

Essence, or life-fire, comes from two sources – our genetic inheritance and the essence we get from the air we breathe and the food and liquid we eat and drink. Any essence we've gathered during the day but not used, is stored in each of our major organs – kidneys, heart, lungs, spleen and liver. However, it is stored mainly in our kidneys which is why the health of the kidneys is so important if you want to live to be 120 years old.

As well as storing essence, the kidneys rule the glands, genitals, reproductive system, bladder organ and function, and fluid distribution in the body. The bladder accepts liquid waste from the kidneys and the heart. Bone marrow is linked to the kidneys, as are problems with the knees, lower back and teeth. Skeletal health is dependant on the overall health of the body, so not every bone problem can be related to the kidneys. The kidneys affect body fluids, so swollen ankles can be attributed to the kidneys, too.

Both kidney yin and kidney yang have important interactive roles with the other organs. Kidney yin reduces heat and sedates the body. It supports, moistens, stabilises and builds tissue. It is the kidney yin that controls the fluids of the body. For example, it is balanced kidney yin that provides enough water for the heart to guard against heart fire, or inflammation of the heart. In winter, especially, pork can tone kidney yin. Try oysters, too.

A major role of kidney yang is the support it provides for the spleen and the lungs. Kidney yang helps and supports the spleen qi to push nutrition upwards. For the lungs, kidney yang moves up to meet lung qi and pull it right down into the body, which ensures oxygen gets to the lower half of the body. If kidney yang is weak, you won't be able to breathe in deeply. Walnuts specifically benefit kidney yang.

The emotion associated with the kidneys is fear. Fear can lead to alienation, the need to be alone and the belief the world isn't safe. In the body, this can manifest as arthritis, deafness and senility.

In our day-to-day lives, the health of our kidneys can be seen in our hair, and experienced through our sense of hearing. Hair loss, premature greying or split ends all signal kidneys that could do with a boost. Many ear problems can be linked to the kidneys, such as ear infections. The health of our kidneys directly impacts on reproduction and sex drive.

The salty flavour

Salt is closely connected to the kidneys. The salty flavour is yin and cooling and moves energy down and in. It has a grounding effect and moistens dryness, softens hardness (such as muscle knots and cataracts), enhances digestion, eases constipation and abdominal swelling, increases appetite, is calming and improves concentration.

Oedema or swelling in the body is usually caused by excessive dampness. However the salty flavour makes oedema worse whereas the bitter flavour can improve the problem and is more suitable for people with damp and also builds the kidneys. For instance, if a person with swollen ankles ate a lot of salt in winter, the symptoms would soon get worse. The best salty foods for people with damp are seaweeds. It is important not to stress the kidneys with too much salt in winter because little salt is lost through sweating when the weather is cold.

Salty foods include crab, crayfish, clams, oysters, mussels, sardines, pork, pork kidney, flake, squid, miso, soy sauce, seaweeds, millet, barley or anything with salt added.

Deficient kidney yin and blood

Winter is the season of regeneration and repair, so is the perfect time to tone the yin. A general yin deficiency, which is not enough fluids in the body to balance the yang or activity of bodily functions, shows up as a line down the centre of the tongue.

A kidney yin deficiency means not enough fluids, especially for the liver, heart and lungs and not enough control over fluids. If kidney yin is not strong enough to control fluids, the result will be disturbed sleep with lots of dreaming. Dreams of water and fish mean kidney yin is flooding the heart. Too much fluid will weaken the heart and drown its fire and passion. If the heart, liver or lungs are out of balance, they may have drawn too heavily on the kidneys and been the cause of the yin deficiency in the kidneys. So any remedy has to balance the whole body.

Some of the symptoms of a general yin deficiency include hypogly-caemia, diabetes, a tendency to thinness, dryness, insomnia, irritability, worry, excess thought and night sweats. When there is a yin deficiency, yang has no counterbalance, so there will often be minor heat signs as well, such as a red tongue. Physical symptoms of kidney yin deficiency include dizziness, ringing in the ears, dry throat and mouth, low back pain, weak legs, spontaneous sweating, a very red tongue. Kidney yin deficiency can lead to kidney yang deficiency and impotence or lack of sex drive.

Insufficient kidney yin can cause problems on several levels. Emotionally, the effects are insecurity and fear. Without strong kidney yin, the personality is not rooted or grounded or dependable and the person has a tendency to move from one issue to the next without getting to the cause of problems. Stressed kidneys hold excess water, which they pass on to the heart. In the heart, the excess water extinguishes the heart fire and the heart's joy and love. So excessive fear blocks love.

The symptoms of menopause are the same as the symptoms of a deficiency of yin fluids, especially those fluids that stabilise and relax the liver. Hot flushes are due to kidney yin deficiency. The heat is from the yang that is without its appropriate counterbalance. The hot flushes and sweating in the upper part of the body happens because the kidney yin isn't strong enough to hold any of the body's heat in the lower body. This also effects liver yin.

To build up yin, eat animal products such as oyster, flake, sardine, crab, clams, eggs, pork, cheese or duck. But only in small amounts so that yin is built up gradually rather than creating mucus and

Walnuts are good for kidney yang, and can ease lumbago. Bake in honey and store in a glass jar. Eat just one, once a day.

•

Oysters combat winter dryness and strengthen yin.

•

Winter pain in the knees, whether it is arthritic or not, can often be eased by foods that support the kidneys since the kidneys affect the knees.

•

Age-old preservation methods such as salting and souring bring the energies of food into the core and are suitable for winter. Try pickles or sauerkraut.

•

Wheat germ is a good general yin toner.

•

To gain strength after sickness, you'll want more concentrated energy. Choose easy to digest, but concentrated foods such as lentils, beans and root vegetables – cook together in a pot with a lid for a longer than usual time.

Mash is comforting in winter. Try mixing potato in a mash with turnip, parsnip, carrot or sweet potato. Add butter and pepper, and use some of the cooking liquid rather than milk to create moisture.

•

When cooking vegetables, use a heavy-based pot with a lid and low heat, and you'll only need a few tablespoons of water or oil to moisten the pot before vegetables start to release their own juices.

•

Pumpkin retains its liquid and more taste if it is steamed or roasted. Keep it out of water.

•

Garlic and peanut cooked together can help arthritis. Simmer a small handful of peanuts and several garlic cloves for an hour and then drink the soup, which will be sweet, as a cure for swelling and damp.

•

In winter, and for people who are weak and cold, choose miso that is darker and has been fermented for a longer time.

blockages in the body that will deplete yin further. To build yin more gradually include rice. Foods for winter that specifically build kidney yin and also build yin for the rest of the body include: beef, barley, turtle beans, mung beans, beetroot, kidney beans, millet, wheat germ, seaweed, black sesame seeds, molasses, spinach, sweet potato and potatoes. Congees, soups or stews naturally support yin.

If you are run-down, you may not be producing enough blood or you may have sluggish circulation. Blood problems include anaemia, vertigo, a tendency to faint, palpitations, nervousness, anxiety attacks, missing periods, lower back pain or night sweats. Blood deficiency is usually caused by a problem with either the spleen or the kidneys. The first thing to do is eat a diet that is easy on the digestive system, so choose warm, well-cooked foods. In winter, foods that nourish and strengthen the blood include pumpkin, beetroot, pork, rice, longan, lotus root, kidney beans, coconut milk and chestnuts.

Deficient kidney yang and qi

Symptoms of a yang deficiency may include cold hands and feet, pale face, mental exhaustion and low spirits, weak knees and lower back pain, low or no sex drive, infertility, irregular periods, clear vaginal discharge, sterility, inability to urinate, clear urine or frequent urination, oedema, asthma, lack of willpower and direction and a large, pale tongue. Typically, a person with deficient kidney yang will have a sedentary lifestyle, be unproductive and struggle making decisions.

While depression is complicated, according to TCM, one of the causes is a deficiency in the kidneys. Kidney yang is the force behind our will to live. If you are always mentally and physically tired and have a sense that everything is just way too hard, the kidney yang may be deficient.

Often the best way to assist the kidney yang is to improve digestion. Eat foods that are well-cooked and easy to digest. Foods that specifically warm kidney yang include cloves, fennel seeds, black pepper, ginger, walnuts, turtle beans, onions, leeks, shallots, chives, chicken, lamb, trout and salmon.

Deficient kidney qi often results in an inability to control urine and semen. Other symptoms of a lack of qi in the kidneys are sore lower back and knees, aching calves or aching on the soles of the feet. All these areas are particularly susceptible to the cold. Parsley can give kidney qi a boost.

So, what to eat in winter?

In winter, we need to eat foods to create warmth, support kidney yin and yang and encourage energy down and in. We also need to eat foods that benefit the heart and shen, guarding against the winter doldrums. And there are winter specialties to enjoy – congees and liqueurs.

Eat warming foods in winter. Soups and stews provide excellent warmth for winter. Warm foods include anchovies, bay leaves, capers, chestnuts, chicken, coriander, dill, fennel, leek, mussels, mutton, nutmeg, pine nuts, rosemary, spring onions, prawns, sweet potatoes and walnuts. Tofu and tempeh and other soy products are very cooling within the body, which in winter is exacerbated by the environment. However, frying tofu and tempeh and then adding to a recipe that includes meat will take the edge off the cold snap.

Foods that benefit the kidneys in winter include sweet potatoes, kidney beans, squid, millet, sesame seeds and lamb. Other good winter foods for the kidneys include turtle beans, black soy beans and brown lentils.

In general, grains, seeds and nuts that have an inward-moving energy are good for winter. However, for children it is important not to overdo grain intake. Because the digestive system is not yet strong and stable, children are likely to develop phlegm if they eat too much grain (especially if it is not very well cooked), which can cause colds, a runny nose, earache and respiratory problems. Especially for younger children, emphasise vegetables or rice congee rather than grains or meat which are harder to digest.

Fruit and raw food or cold food and drinks can also make things worse and cause diarrhoea in children. Both children and adults with heat or damp should be careful to limit nut intake. Nuts are best for people needing to gain strength and moisture. Remember to chew nuts very well as otherwise they can be too hard on the digestive system.

Both salty and bitter flavours are good for winter as they encourage energy to move down and in. Although most people can use salt, people with damp can choose bitter foods instead. Salty foods tend to moisten internal dryness, which can be a problem for some people. Salty flavours for winter include crab, crayfish, clams, oysters, mussels, sardines, pork, pork kidney, flake, squid, miso, soy sauce, seaweeds, millet and barley. Of course, for people trying to limit their salt intake, it's better to add less salt to your food rather then forego clams or oysters!

Since bitter foods enter the heart before they enter any other organ, they are also important in supporting the heart and shen against feeling down in winter. People with bone problems should limit their intake of bitter foods, as should anyone who is deficient, weak, cold, thin or dry. For a bitter taste in winter, add turnip, celery, citrus peel, rye or oats to a meal. Beetroot is a winter food that strengthens the heart qi and the blood.

In winter, it's good to have a richer diet because the cold temperature and cold wind is very drying. Use pork and silver beet cooked with two figs to moisten the lungs in cold weather. In winter, there is a direct attack on the skin and the nose, and the lungs and wei qi (immunity) have an extra workload. If we get run-down, our lungs can become inflamed and then catch cold. Kidneys are the children of the lungs (according to the mother–child relationship), and when the lungs are weak, the kidneys become weak too and we are more susceptible to the cold.

As always, it is essential to eat foods that support the spleen and stomach. Foods such as cabbage, pumpkin, potatoes, yams, sweet potato, carrots, and oats help the stomach and spleen work together. For general digestive support try pumpkin or sweet potato soup made with lamb or chicken or turkey stock. If there are no signs of heat in the body (such as yellow coating on the tongue), add ginger, cardamom, cinnamon, or nutmeg. Winter foods that drain damp include barley, adzuki beans, anchovies, chestnuts, chicken, clams, Job's tears barley, kidney beans, kohlrabi, parsnip, tuna, prawns and turnip.

In winter, sourdough rye bread with liver paté makes the perfect light breakfast or lunch. Rye is naturally bitter and good for the heart. The baking process also makes it sour, which makes the bread good for the liver. Rye dries damp, builds strength and muscles and aids digestion. Liver, within the paté, strengthens both the liver and kidneys.

•

Vegetable stock packs a punch if you experiment a little. Tied in muslin cloth, add star anise, liquorice root, cloves, fennel seeds and a mandarin peel to your next stock.

•

Cooking methods that are slow, use low heat and leave the food unmoved during the process, tend to produce food that has a calming effect when eaten.

•

To improve concentration for studying, eat warm, simple meals with only a couple of ingredients. To enhance sociability, eat light meals with more ingredients.

Many of the ingredients that can be added to congee have similar if not as strong effects when included in the diet in other ways.

•

To properly combine food essences in the cooking process takes a long time. This may seem strange to people used to being told that the less food is cooked, the healthier it is. Sometimes the body needs extra help and combining the essences of foods can do that.

•

Try to cook anything that has to simmer for more than an hour in a clay pot.

•

Eating liver is an effective way to support the liver and eating kidneys is an effective way to support the kidneys.

•

Many women with low iron feel the cold sooner and more extremely than women with normal iron levels. Many of the foods recommended by TCM for winter (such as seaweed, legumes and beef) are naturally high in iron.

In winter, warm pungents remove cold. Because of their connection with the lungs, pungents keep the lungs in good health even though the weather is cold and we tend to do less exercise. Warm pungents for winter include rosemary, shallots, garlic, onions, cinnamon, cloves, ginger, black pepper, fennel, anise, dill and horseradish. If you have signs of heat, use neutral pungents, such as taro, turnip and kohlrabi.

As spring is the next season, it is important to prepare the liver. Foods to remove liver stagnancy in winter include livers (or paté), mussels, horse-radish, fennel, cabbage, turnip, beetroot, bay leaf, taro, cauliflower, broccoli, brussel sprouts, ginger and kohlrabi. Bitter and sour foods will reduce liver excess. Try dandelion root or grape-fruit. The best foods to cool and detoxify the liver in winter are rhubarb, daikon radish, beetroot and cabbage. Foods to reduce liver wind symp-toms in winter include fennel, ginger and oats.

Eating liver builds yin and blood, and it helps prepare the body for spring. Whenever you cook liver, cook it very lightly so that it doesn't become tough.

Winter is an excellent season to try the time-honoured tradition of congee. Congee, or rice water, is a slow-cooked rice porridge (or some-times made with wheat or millet or oats) that is traditionally eaten for breakfast by many Chinese.

Other ingredients are added depending on the health needs of each person. One part rice is added to a heavy-based pot with four parts water, plus another ingredient – depending on the type of congee you want. The mix is then gently cooked for three to six hours. The longer it cooks, the more thoroughly the ingredients blend with the rice, which ensures the healing properties can be full ingested. In the 1970s, the 'crockpot' was perfect for congee making. Now the same thing is available under the name 'slow cooker' and it means you can cook congee overnight.

Some common congee ingredients include:

adzuki beans – remove damp and ease swelling

carrot – eases indigestion

celery – calms liver and treats high blood pressure

chestnut – strengthens kidneys, lower back and knees

fennel – eases flatulence and removes clotting during menstruation

kidney – strengthens kidneys and helps with lower back pain and sexual problems

leek – warms the body and counteracts chronic diarrhoea

liver – nourishes blood and treats liver deficiency (when the liver is balanced there is less anger and irritability) – add liver mixed with a little sugar and salt only in the last minutes of cooking

mung beans – cools summer heat and reduces fever

pine nuts – builds the yin of the heart and lungs

radish – cools heat from the digestive system

sesame seeds – moisten the intestines and treat arthritis

spinach – acts as a sedative and eases burping and acid regurgitation

Winter is the time to enjoy an alcoholic beverage in moderation. Wine is pungent and bitter and sweet and enlivens the spleen, warms the digestive system, expels wind and cold, promotes circulation of the qi and blood, improves appetite and dispels fatigue. It is dry and warm or hot and can be used to dispel dampness and cold. Its yang nature enables

Avoid sitting too long with a full stomach as this can lead to sluggish digestion. After a big meal, take a walk of three hundred steps.
– Professor Lun Wong

•

In winter, some of the best fish include ling, orange roughy and warehou (which is also known as trevally).

•

The qi in food depends on how the food was grown, stored and cooked.

•

Toast for breakfast? For a change, try rye sourdough toast with paté, hummus, cheese, miso paste or tahini, or rice congee with varied ingredients.

•

Having miso soup? Crack an egg into it and stir for extra texture.

•

Add a teaspoon of cider vinegar to speed cooking of beans or a stew. It adds real bite to the taste as well.

•

Some strong pungents such as garlic, mugwort and cayenne expel or destroy parasites.

these positive effects to reach everywhere in the body including the head, skin and extremities. It is particularly useful when the weather is windy, cold, raining and damp. In moderation, alcohol is a great tonic as we get older. And a little wine can add to good times with friends – which is important.

Alcohol is also poisonous – so only drink amounts your particular body is comfortable with. Drinking too much will impair the mind, blood, stomach and increase production of phlegm-fire. The yang nature of alcohol means that if you go to sleep immediately after drinking or when drunk, too much heat is trapped in the body. This heat is harmful to the eyes and heart – which explains the red eyes. The bad mood and headache is linked to the liver. People suffering from diseases of the gallbladder, liver, kidney or from fever should completely avoid alcohol.

Winter is the season of the medicinal liqueur. Alcohol speeds up the actions of any herb it is mixed with. Mixed with herbs, the alcohol delivers a fast-acting pick-me-up. You'll need to create your medicinal liqueurs up to a month in advance to allow time for the herbs to soak in the alcohol sufficiently. Typically, vodka is the best alcohol to use as a base for liqueurs because it is neutral, whereas the junipers used to make gin could change or harm the added herbs.

Winter recipes

Liqueur for indigestion and regurgitation

250 ml rice wine

10 g cardamom, crushed

5 g hawthorn fruit (shan zha)

Combine all ingredients in a glass container. Soak for a week to ten days. Strain and discard solids. Take one teaspoonful twice a day with a glass of warm water.

Liqueur for the common cold with a headache and mild fever

60 g chrysanthemum flowers

60 g wolfberry (gou qi zi)

200 ml vodka

20 g honey

Soak the chrysanthemums and wolfberry in the vodka in a glass container for between two and three weeks. Add the honey and, when necessary, take one teaspoon twice a day.

Tendon tonic

SERVES I

Tendons are very good for the qi, liver and to build the blood. Peanuts are very moistening and, if simmered slowly, will soften the chewiness of the tendons. This dish is very good for counteracting anaemia.

100 g beef tendons

150 g peanuts, outer shell removed but brown inner skin intact

Add tendons and peanuts to eight cups of water, cover and simmer for several hours. Serve with steamed rice.

Rabbit tonic

FOR ANYONE FEELING WEAK

Rabbit is sweet and cold. It builds the qi and the body yin, improving the appetite and strength and quenching thirst, especially for people with diabetes.

Meat from one rabbit

100 g shan yao (Chinese yam)

Boil enough water to cover rabbit. Add rabbit and shan yao. Cover and simmer slowly until the meat is tender. Eat the meat and drink the soup.

Walnut and chicken soup

SERVES 4

This dish builds yang for the whole body and specifically tones the kidneys. It builds the body, clears the mind and improves memory. This dish may help improve such conditions as impotence, blurred vision and too-frequent urination. Avoid this dish if you have a cold, fever or diarrhoea.

125 g walnuts
1 chicken (young)
1 piece mandarin skin
10 g rou cong rong (cistanche)
pinch of salt

Soak walnuts in one litre of water for half an hour and make sure all skin is rubbed off. Boil chicken in water for five minutes. Discard water, remove flesh from the bones and cut meat into bite-sized pieces. In a clay pot, add all ingredients except salt. Bring to the boil, then cover and simmer for two hours. Add salt and serve.

Shank soup with dang gui

SERVES 1

Dang gui nourishes the blood and improves circulation, supports the heart and helps with health problems such as anaemia, menstrual irregularities, injuries and arthritis. This dish can also strengthen the body, improve sleep and warm and ease lower back pain, asthma, anaemia and poor appetite.

1 small lamb shank

$^1/_2$ teaspoon salt

1 teaspoon finely chopped shallots

1 knob fresh ginger

2 chopped walnuts

5 Chinese red dates (da zao or jujube)

10 g dang gui

10 g dried longan, finely chopped

1 star anise

freshly ground black pepper

1 tablespoon rice wine

splash tamari

Place shank and salt in a saucepan and cover with water. Simmer covered for an hour, allow to cool and scoop off any fat that rises to the surface. Remove shank from the liquid and use a fork to push off the meat in small pieces. Break up any larger pieces. Put bone aside and return meat to the saucepan. Add shallots and ginger, bring to the boil and simmer for ten minutes. Add everything else except wine and tamari and simmer for another ten minutes. Remove the ginger and dang gui root. Add tamari and wine and serve.

Blood-building soup

SERVES I

This is a simpler version of SHANK SOUP WITH DANG GUI. While both beef and lamb are warm-natured, once in the body, they move in different directions. The warmth from beef moves up to warm the upper part of the body, whereas the warmth from lamb moves down towards the kidneys and the genital area. Lamb's downward flow is especially good for the kidney yang.

Cook this soup to build the blood in winter, especially for women whose periods have stopped or are irregular. This dish will also clear wind and cold and increase strength and blood (rather than the qi, which makes it very good for women). Other symptoms this soup may ease include palpitations, insomnia, cold limbs and difficulty getting pregnant. This soup shouldn't be taken by anyone with a cold or fever.

10 g dang gui

150 g lean lamb

6 black dates with stones removed

100 g dried longan

100 g ginger

pinch of salt

Steam dang gui, then finely slice it. Boil lamb in water for five minutes then discard water and chop off any obvious fat. In enough fresh water to cover all the ingredients by two centimetres, reboil the lamb. Add all other ingredients except salt, cover and simmer for three hours. Add a little salt and serve with rice.

Cauliflower soup

Soup stock is an excellent way to get the benefits of meat for people who usually avoid it. This dish will remove stagnancy from the liver, improve mood and brighten the eyes, enhance energy levels, clear heat from the lungs and warm the body, especially the lower body. Omit the cheese if you have a mucus condition.

1 litre lamb or mutton stock

1 cauliflower, with stem sliced and head broken into small pieces

2 teaspoons miso (darker miso for colder climates)

small handful chopped parsley

freshly ground black pepper

12 thin slices parmesan cheese (optional)

In the stock, cook cauliflower until tender. Stir though miso. Puree soup, then add parsley and pepper. (For a chunkier soup, don't puree – gently use a vegetable masher instead.) If desired, place two slices of cheese in the middle of each bowl and serve.

Fried fennel and potato with bacon

If the heavier foods of winter have given you an extra dose of flatulence, get rid of it with fennel. It is also good for menstrual pain caused by cold or stagnation in winter. This dish is quite warming, so people with hypertension may wish to leave out the bacon. Pungents, such as fennel, relax the nervous system in winter.

1 bulb fennel

2 potatoes, boiled

2 tablespoons olive oil

2 rashers smoked streaky bacon

1 teaspoon fennel seeds

1 knob turmeric, chopped

1 knob ginger, chopped

freshly ground pepper

Boil the fennel for 20 minutes until it is tender. Drain well and chop into small pieces. Chop potato into quite small but similar sized pieces and mix with fennel. With the smallest amount of oil in a non-stick frying pan, cook bacon. Cut bacon into small pieces and add bacon and fennel seeds to the potato and fennel mix. In the frying pan with remaining bacon fat, sizzle turmeric and ginger. Tip all other ingredients back into the pan. Cook for 15 minutes, remembering to stir to avoid sticking and burning. To serve, add a twist of freshly ground pepper.

Beetroot mush

This will bring some colour to your winter palette. You can mix and match with almost any seasonal vegetable you have on hand. It supports the heart, blood, digestive system and kidneys. It also removes damp, especially if you choose to add the adzuki beans. Your mood, hair and complexion should all show the benefits.

1 cup white rice

1 tablespoon olive oil

1 small knob ginger, finely chopped

2 beetroot, chopped

2 carrots, chopped

1 large parsnip, chopped

1 cup cooked lentils, red kidney beans or adzuki beans

1 tablespoon shoyu

Cover rice with water and a lid and cook using the absorption method (see page 46) or use a rice cooker. Heat wok, add oil. When oil is hot, add ginger and sauté for two minutes. Add beetroot, carrots and parsnip and stir. Add a dash of boiling water to stop sticking until vegetables give up their own juice. Reduce heat and cover, leaving vegetables to steam in their own juices for 25 minutes. Add lentils or beans and shoyu and stir through until the lentils are hot. Serve in deep bowls with rice and vegetables mixed thoroughly together.

Sweet hearts

SERVES 2

After giving birth, a woman's body is like an empty nest. The void left by the baby is cold, so the mother should avoid all cold foods and build her strength. Pig's trotter cooked in black rice vinegar and ginger is the traditional recuperation dish. It helps with general recuperation and to increase milk flow for the lactating mother. Like pig's trotters, this dish is good for a woman who has recently given birth. It can also benefit people with a kidney yin deficiency.

1 onion

1 potato

2 carrots

150 g pumpkin

150 g sliced cabbage

2 tablespoons sesame oil

250 g chicken gizzards and hearts

$^1/_2$ cup cooking sherry

$^1/_2$ teaspoon honey

$^1/_2$ teaspoon cardamom

$^1/_2$ teaspoon cinnamon

250 g tomato paste

3 thin slices fresh ginger

extra sesame oil

Dice vegetables. Heat oil in a frying pan or wok. Add onion and meat and stir frequently until the onions are clear and the meat starts to turn brown. Transfer to a thick-based saucepan (cast iron or stainless steel is good). Add all the other ingredients and stir everything through. Cover ingredients with water. Bring to the boil and then cover and simmer for $1^1/_2$ hours. Stir occasionally and add more water if necessary. After serving into individual bowls dribble a little sesame oil over each portion.

Baked vegetables

This simple dish supports and calms the liver, relieving mild depression, frustration and anger. It also dries damp, strengthens the heart, supports the blood, warms the body and enhances digestion. People with damp will benefit most from including mainly unsalted pistachios, pumpkin seeds and linseed in the nut mix.

1 small onion, finely chopped

1 clove garlic, crushed

1 teaspoon olive oil

3 carrots, halved

4 parsnips, in big chunks

6 small beetroot

3 potatoes, halved

3 small kohlrabi, cut in half (if not available substitute turnip)

5 tablespoons nuts and seeds, ground

1 teaspoon kelp powder

2 teaspoons cinnamon

1 tablespoon soy sauce

Heat oven to 180°C. In a wok over medium heat, sauté onion and garlic in oil until clear. Add root vegetables, continue to sauté for another five minutes. In a bowl, thoroughly mix all other ingredients with $3/4$ cup of water to create a gravy. Transfer vegetables from frying pan to a lightly oiled baking dish. Cover with gravy. Cover with lid and bake for an hour, when vegetables should be soft enough to easily penetrate with a fork. Serve.

Marinated mussels

Mussels build energy, essence and blood. Your liver and kidneys will appreciate this dish and you'll feel more vital. Make sure all ingredients are very fresh.

24 mussels

2 bay leaves

large sprig thyme

2 cups white wine

2 cups olive oil

$1/2$ cup apple cider vinegar

1 cup parsley, chopped

$1/2$ cup shallots, finely chopped

Put mussels in a wide frying pan. Add bay leaves and thyme. Cover the bottom of the pan with white wine. Cover and steam using high heat. After five minutes, noisy steam will indicate the mussels are opening. Remove the opened mussels and give those that remain another couple of minutes of steam. Discard those that remain closed. Remove top of shell from each mussel. Mix oil and vinegar, and add parsley and shallots. Tip enough liquid on to each mussel to marinate. Serve after 30 minutes.

White eel

This dish is especially good for anyone suffering with arthritis. Eel meat assists liver and kidney deficiency and nourishes the blood. It clears wind and damp from the joints and should ease arthritic pain. To explain it a bit further, the health and functions of the liver and kidneys affects the qi and the blood, and when the blood is deficient, it doesn't fill up the vessels properly and leaves air pockets which can be seen as internal wind. Damp in the joints also relates to stagnation and insufficient nourishment delivered via the blood.

1 white eel, washed and cut into 2 cm pieces

2 teaspoons brandy or whisky

2 teaspoons sambuca (or other sweet black alcohol)

2 teaspoons brown vinegar

6 thin slices ginger

1 tablespoon olive oil

pinch of salt

Dry fry eel in a wok or frying pan to remove any water from washing, then add other ingredients and fry gently for approximately 20 minutes until tender. Serve with steamed rice.

Lentil–walnut bake

This dish provides support to the heart and kidneys. Physically, it warms, strengthens and comforts. Emotionally, foods such as lentils and walnuts help us feel grounded and able to cope. The rising pungency of wheat germ helps lift depression and stagnancy that causes frustration and irritability.

$^1/_2$ onion, finely chopped

1 teaspoon olive oil

2 cups cooked lentils

$^1/_2$ cup wheat germ

$^1/_2$ cup whole-wheat breadcrumbs

$^1/_2$ cup walnuts, chopped

$^1/_2$ teaspoon dry sage or 1 teaspoon chopped fresh sage

$^1/_2$ cup lentil broth or vegetable stock

1 tablespoon apple cider vinegar

pinch of salt

Preheat oven to 180°C. Sauté onions in oil. Combine with other ingredients and pack into a large loaf dish that has been pre-oiled. Cover, and bake for 30 minutes. Remove cover and cook for a further ten minutes. Serve.

Cabbage leaves seasoned with pork, livers and chestnuts

SERVES 4

Cabbage is a wonder food with a bad name. Try eating it to warm chronically cold feet, ease depression and improve digestion. If you are overweight or have damp, replace the mashed potatoes with a mixed mash of sweet potato and turnips. For excessive heat (especially in the upper body) or high cholesterol, replace the minced pork with cooked rice mixed with rosemary. If you tend to be weak with a pale tongue, add one or two slices of ginger, finely diced.

leaves 1 cabbage, blanched and drained
cotton to tie leaves
3 leeks, sliced
1 carrot, sliced
1 clove garlic, crushed
3 bay leaves
1 sprig thyme
3 cups stock

SEASONING
250 g minced pork
8 chicken livers, finely sliced
6 roasted chestnuts
$^1/_2$ cup fresh breadcrumbs
1 teaspoon cinnamon, anise, nutmeg or cardamom or a blend
$^1/_2$ teaspoon salt
freshly ground black pepper
1 egg
2 tablespoons freshly chopped parsley
1 teaspoon freshly chopped thyme
olive oil

Preheat oven to 180°C. Mix seasoning ingredients, except thyme and parsley, and cook in olive oil in a covered wok for ten minutes, stirring occasionally. Remove from heat, and add thyme and parsley. Spread cabbage leaves out on the bench, divide seasoning so there is an equal amount for each leaf. Place seasoning on leaf and wrap it up, tucking in the ends of the leaf. Then tie each bundle with cotton. Place bundles in a cast-iron baking dish in a tight layer with the seam underneath, and put the sliced leek and carrot on top, along with the garlic, bay leaves and thyme. Use a dish small enough so the bundles are packed in tightly for support. Pour the stock over the bundles. Cover with a lid and bake for 45 minutes. Serve with mashed potatoes or rice.

Stir-fried daikon radish loupou with carrot

SIDE DISH

This is a great dish for the spleen. The carrot supports digestion and the daikon radish dries damp that hinders digestion.

Heat wok and add sesame oil. When oil is hot, add finely chopped daikon radish and carrot. Stir-fry. When carrots and radish are just done, add a handful of chopped shallots and cook for another minute. Add shoyu or black pepper to taste and serve.

Pork with black bean

SERVES 4

This is a very building dish. It builds qi and improves memory and is especially good for anyone who is thin and dry. It nourishes the lungs, spleen, stomach and blood and acts as a sedative. This dish can ease palpitations, shortness of breath, weakness in the limbs or loose bowels. As this dish builds the blood, it should be avoided by people who tend to bleed excessively, such as people who suffer regular nosebleeds.

Dang shen is a Chinese herb. Its effect is similar to ginseng, without being as heating.

In the past, the cut of meat considered best for this recipe was the pig's tail.

8 Chinese red dates (da zao or jujube)
salt
400 g pork in one piece, with a little fat still attached
30 g black beans, soaked
30 g dang shen (pilose asiabell root)
1 piece mandarin skin
1 piece ginger

Soak red dates for half an hour to make it easier to remove the stones. Salt pork very finely. Cook black beans in a dry wok until they pop and split. Remove from heat and run under cold water. In a clay cooking pot, bring 1^1/$_2$ litres of water to the boil. Gradually add ingredients so water doesn't stop boiling for long at any point. When all ingredients (including beans) are in the pot and water is boiling, turn down heat, cover and simmer for three hours. Serve with rice.

Cooked brains

SERVES I

Tian Ma is a great herb for calming wind symptoms, specifically in the liver. Wolfberry (gou qi zi) builds liver and kidney yin, blood and eyesight. This dish is especially good for anyone experiencing dizziness, tinnitus (ringing in the ears), loss of memory, rheumatoid arthritis or blurred vision. All of these symptoms point to a weakness or deficiency of yin, especially in the liver and kidney yin. However, if you suffer from high cholesterol, only have this dish once a month.

1 pork or lamb brain
salt
10 g tian ma (gastrodia tuber)
10 g wolfberry (gou qi zi)

Soak the brain in cold, salted water and leave in the refrigerator for several hours, then remove all blood vessels and the membrane. In fresh water, add a pinch of salt and soak in the refrigerator again for an hour. Remove the brain from the water and place in a bowl suitable for steaming (not aluminium), add the tian ma and wolfberry and pour in two cups of boiling water. Steam over pot of simmering water for approximately $1^1/_4$ hours.

Serve in a bowl with some of the stock poured over the brain. Add shoyu to taste and use steamed rice as the accompaniment.

To enjoy brain fritters: soak, clean and poach brains in vegetable stock for five minutes. Then dip in a mixture of egg, milk, pepper and spices. Roll in breadcrumbs and fry.

Adzuki bars

Adzuki beans are legendary driers of damp – not a good choice if you are dry, but excellent if you want to remove damp that may be causing arthritis, lethargy, depression or excess weight. The other ingredients enhance the dish's calming qualities and should make for an enjoyable snack.

1 cup adzuki beans, soaked

1 vanilla bean, split lengthways

3 cups apple juice

$^1/_2$ cup carob powder

1 cup apple sauce

$^1/_2$ cup rice flour

1 cup whole-wheat flour

$^1/_2$ teaspoon salt

1 teaspoon cinnamon

1 tablespoon tahini

$^1/_2$ cup chopped pistachio nuts (unsalted)

$^1/_2$ cup sultanas

Cook adzuki beans with vanilla bean and apple juice until the beans are soft – about 1$^1/_2$ hours. Discard vanilla bean and mash adzuki beans. Preheat oven to 180°C, oil a slice tray and place in oven. Mix all other ingredients in with bean mash and pour mixture into the oiled slice tray. Bake for 1$^1/_4$ hours until top crust is firm. Allow to cool. Cut and serve.

CHAPTER EIGHT

Ingredients

This list of ingredients describes some of the attributes TCM links with particular foods. However, it is neither all-inclusive nor exhaustive – that would take several books. As there can be many causes of a simple complaint such as a headache, the foods listed as being appropriate to ease a headache will not fix every headache. Consider what may be causing your particular headache. Take into account your body type, the environment, your diet, your stress levels and the season. Think of your body and mind as an integrated system – and if you have a serious health issue, seek professional help.

What this list aims to do is show how the foods we eat play such an important role in our wellbeing. Think of it as a teaser – an encouragement to eat widely of the freshest and best quality foods available in your area each season. Use it in unison with the seasonal charts to make the most out of your meals and get the best from your life.

Adzuki beans are sweet and sour, warming and remove damp. They clear heat and remove toxins by freeing up urination which benefits the kidneys. (They are especially good to treat a bladder infection.) Adzuki beans also alleviate swelling and calm skin infections. Adzuki beans are useful for anyone with diarrhoea and people wanting to lose weight.

Alfalfa is bitter, cooling and dries damp. Alfalfa treats swelling, arthritis, bloating and aids weight loss. Alfalfa also clears heat from the spleen and stomach and may ease alcohol addiction.

Almonds are warm and sweet and affect the lungs and the large intestines. They moisten the lungs, reduce phlegm, make breathing easier and ease coughing. Almonds also remove blockages and counteract dryness in the large intestine. If you have chronic damp and swelling or distension of the abdomen, avoid almonds as they will aggravate symptoms.

Aloe vera is bitter and cold, and helps clear heat in and out of the body. Internally, aloe treats heat-related headaches, dizziness, tinnitus (ringing in the ears), insomnia and constipation. Externally, aloe can ease sunburn, insect bites and burns. It is best avoided when pregnant.

Apples are cool and sweet – the autumn antidote to the remains of summer heat. Apples tone blood and qi and sedate yang. As autumn is the season in which we often experience internal dryness, and the season associated with the lungs, apples are particularly useful at this time because they produce fluid within the body. This fluid lubricates and moistens the lungs. This can be particularly helpful to people who are wanting to start the repair process after giving up smoking cigarettes. Apples can also be helpful if you have indigestion, a hangover or morning sickness.

> Apple syrup is a good cordial in faintings, palpitations, and melancholy. – Nicholas Culpepper, 1653

Apricots moisten and strengthen the lungs, calm panting and ease asthma. They are also good for dry mouths and dry throats and coughs, and constipation caused by dryness. If you seem to be unable to quite catch your breath in summer, try an apricot.

Asparagus is cold, sweet and bitter. It counterbalances heat caused by the environment and generated in the body. Many foods that dry damp tend to dry out the organs as well, however, asparagus dries damp while also lubricating dryness. The kidneys and the arteries benefit from the clearing qualities of asparagus. Asparagus is also helpful for clearing the lungs, so if you eat asparagus in the spring and summer, your lungs will be in good shape to face autumn when it arrives. On the other hand, if your tongue is showing signs of cold, don't overdo the asparagus intake.

Astragalus or huang qi is a sweet, warm herb that strengthens the protective qi. Especially at night, it stops perspiration by closing the skin's pores which helps wei qi (our immune system) to protect the body. Astragalus speeds up the healing process and reduces swelling. In winter, add a little to soups as a tonic for qi if you are recovering from sickness and are still feeling washed out.

Avocado is cooling and sweet. It builds blood and yin and increases fluid in the lungs and intestines. Avocado calms the liver and eases feelings of anger and irritation.

Bananas are cold and sweet. They are one of the few fruits that tone yin. The cold nature of bananas helps them clear heat. This is useful if you are a hot-type person, whereas if you are a damp or cold-type person, eating bananas won't be helpful. Bananas tone qi and blood and lubricate the intestines, which is good if you have a tendency to constipation. Specifically, soft bananas can relieve constipation, while almost ripe bananas relieve diarrhoea. Another important property of bananas is that they clear toxins from the body and are often used to treat alcoholism. If you have stomach pain, avoid bananas.

Barley is sweet, salty and cooling. It gives you physical strength, boosts energy, cools and builds the blood, fortifies the spleen and gets rid of accumulations, which are all beneficial for anyone who is bruising easily. Barley supports yin and moistens dryness, disperses swelling, clears bright yellowness from urine and is very soothing. Barley can be good if you have indigestion or diarrhoea. Boiled and drunk as a tea, barley relieves heat and fatigue.

Basil is good for almost everything, as long as you have healthy qi. Basil removes blood stagnation, disperses wind, expels cold, transforms damp and counteracts toxins. It calms the liver, helps get rid of menstrual clotting and lessens abdominal swelling, distension, skin eruptions (such as acne) and the tendency to burp.

Bay leaf is the perfect addition to winter stews. It pushes cold out of the body, removes blood stagnation and regulates and strengthens qi. Regulating qi is just as important as strengthening it because if energy in our bodies is strong but moving in the wrong direction, or in fits and starts, it can do more damage than good. Bay leaf can be used to treat itching and skin eruptions.

Beef is building and enriches the yin. Qi, blood, fluids, tendons and bones are all beneficiaries of beef. A yin deficiency may be the reason for aches in the lower back or feeling weak in the knees, so eating the occasional serve of beef can be very helpful. Anyone not getting enough food, such as people recovering from anorexia, will quickly feel better if a small amount of beef is added to their diet. However, if you have external injuries or skin disease, avoid eating beef.

Beef kidneys are sweet and directly benefit the kidneys. Impotence, poor sex drive, lumbago (lower back pain), weak knees and bones, problem hearing and poor hair condition may be improved by occasionally adding beef kidneys to the diet.

Beef liver strengthens qi, blood and the liver. As the eyes are related to the function of the liver, tired eyes, night-blindness and blurred vision can be helped with beef liver.

Beetroot is sweet and strengthens the heart, calms the spirit, purifies the blood, clears and tones the liver, supports yin and regulates menstruation. It treats hardening of the arteries, arthritis, liver stagnation and can ease some symptoms of menopause, especially when eaten with carrot.

Black beans are sweet and warming. Black beans act as a blood tonic, support yin and warm the lower back and pelvic region. They can be very helpful to treat infertility and can be beneficial for women who experience painful periods or anyone with kidney weakness or lumbago. There are two types of black beans. Those that originated in Mexico are also called turtle beans and are members of the kidney bean family and need to be soaked overnight and cooked for several hours. Black beans used in Asian cooking are already fermented and can be soaked for ten minutes before being rinsed and added to the cooking pot.

Black pepper is hot. It expels cold, damp, stagnation and warms the stomach and spleen. Black pepper sends energy downwards in the body, which helps calm the liver qi, and is good for hypertension which is a result of rising liver qi (as long as there is no heat in the body). Check your tongue and, as long as it is not bright red with a yellow coating, black pepper is good for the liver and may be helpful if you are feeling angry or frustrated, or if you have hiccups, indigestion or diarrhoea or if you are vomiting clear liquid.(See also PEPPER)

Black sesame tones qi and blood and lubricates all the zang organs – the heart, lungs, spleen, liver and kidneys. As long as your stomach and spleen are in good working order, black sesame is extremely nutritious. Eat black sesame to brighten the eyes, shine the hair and for an extra boost to delay premature greying of the hair. However, if you are ninety, there will be no miracles! (See also SESAME)

Black soybeans are less cooling, with a stronger action than yellow varieties. They improve circulation and water use within the body. They help get rid of wind and toxins in the body and treat abdominal swelling and skin eruptions such as acne. (See also SOYBEANS)

Broad beans are sweet supporters of the spleen and digestion process. They help remove damp, reduce swelling and ease diarrhoea.

Broccoli is pungent and slightly bitter and helps our bodies cope with heat. It is cooling and especially good for hot, red eyes, which it brightens. If you feel bothered by heat, or have difficulty urinating, try eating this greenest of flowers.

Buckwheat is cool and sweet with descending energy. It clears heat, improves appetite and lowers rebellious qi, which improves digestion. Buckwheat strengthens blood vessels and improves circulation to the hands and feet, so it can be very beneficial during the colder months. However, buckwheat shouldn't be used by anyone who has excess wind problems such as vertigo.

Wind is often caused, or generated, by heat. As heat rises from the liver it can cause dizziness (wind) in the head.

Butter is warm and sweet. It can be used to treat body odour and skin eruptions and is strengthening for the qi and blood, especially for people with few animal products in their diet.

Cabbage is sweet and pungent. In winter, when there is less light and less activity, more people experience depression than at any other time of the year. Cabbage is one of a number of foods that help to relieve mental depression. In winter, cook cabbage for longer than normal to clear damp. Cabbage promotes digestion and removes heat from the digestive system. It can also treat stomach ulcers.

It's best not to eat Chinese cabbage if you already feel even a little nauseous. Cabbage also helps disperse heat-based inflammation such as rashes, red and irritated eyes or a sore throat. Regularly including cabbage in your diet can warm chronically cold feet. And cabbage can help get rid of an alcoholic thirst. There are many varieties of cabbage – experiment.

Cabbage has been cultivated in Europe since 400 BCE and was a food the Romans thought could stop them feeling the effects of overindulging on alcohol. Dioscorides recognised it as a digestive aid. Traditional Chinese practitioners share both these views.

Cantaloupe is cooling in the summer heat, as is honeydew melon.

Capers are warm and ascending in nature which gets things moving up and out. On the out list is dampness, wind, cold and stagnant blood. This clearing quality means capers can be particularly useful for anyone who has been leading a sedentary life or for anyone who has rheumatoid arthritis.

Cardamom is warming without being heating and is very gentle on the stomach and spleen. The subtlety of cardamom clears the digestive system and may ease acid regurgitation, nausea, vomiting, indigestion, abdominal swelling, gastritis, diarrhoea and loss of appetite. During pregnancy, cardamom can be used to calm the foetus. And cardamom helps ease a hangover.

When drinking carrot juice, people with liver stagnation or dampness can add a little green from the carrot tops to counteract the sweetness that could make these symptoms worse.

Carrots are sweet, splendid spleen food. They strengthen the spleen and give the digestion system enough oomph to clear away undigested remains from previous meals, as well as accumulations within the body. Cooked carrots can be used to improve any digestion problem. When the spleen is working well, the body is more likely to turn food into muscle rather than fat. Carrots also strengthen the lungs and the liver function.

Unlike many vegetables, mature carrots are usually sweeter than their immature counterparts – choose the big ones for your dinner.

Cauliflower is a winter vegetable from the same family as cabbage, kohlrabi and broccoli. Although cauliflower and many other foods have not been studied by traditional Chinese practitioners, you can make assumptions based on other similar foods that have been studied.

Cayenne pepper is hot. Use it sparingly and it will boost your energy. When the weather is very cold, and yin is naturally strong, we may lack the motivation to get things done. This pepper gives yang a kick-start. Cayenne pepper is a good remedy for the overexposure to cold and wet that can cause chilblains.

Celery is cool. In the 1960s, when dudes said 'cool it' to mean calm down, they could have been referring to celery. Or maybe not. But celery's cooling effects are felt on the liver, which is home to the emotion of anger. Celery cools and brings heat down throughout the body. Whenever heat or wind get out of hand, celery can help with headaches, vertigo, nervousness, conjunctivitis, arthritis, high blood pressure, red face and eyes, bladder infections or swelling. Celery also benefits the spleen, dries damp and controls appetite. As celery calms and strengthens the liver, the effects will be obvious in your eyes and fingernails and your tendons will be stronger, so you'll be less likely to injure yourself.

The ancient Romans believed wearing celery as a wreath around the head could help ease a hangover.

Cherries dispel wind from the body. As their colour suggests, cherries nourish the blood and get it moving more strongly which is great if you have poor circulation or numbness, especially in the limbs. Cherries are good for anyone suffering with rheumatic pains. After the inactivity of winter, wind can infiltrate the spaces in the body where nothing else is happening, so foods such as cherries get things moving internally, shake us out of the winter doldrums and prepare us for the activity of summer. Cherries also treat anaemia and support the spleen.

Chestnuts are warm and sweet when roasted – the perfect snack for winter. They assist yang, expel cold and nourish the stomach and spleen. If you've been feeling nauseous or have watery diarrhoea or nosebleeds, chestnuts are perfect. Chestnuts are also good for the kidneys and, if you've been feeling weak in the knees or lower back, chestnuts can give you a lift. As well as roasted chestnuts, try chestnut congee. As with other foods that directly support the kidneys, the benefits of eating chestnuts will reflect in your hair.

In the past in China, male chickens were often castrated to promote growth in the bird. It was considered very bad for the health to eat a bird which had been castrated but continued to give the early morning crow – as the job had only been half done.

Chicken is warm and sweet and strengthening for the spleen and stomach. It is useful for building up energy in someone who is weak, such as people recovering from illness or anorexia or struggling to regain their strength after childbirth. Chicken also removes stagnation in the blood, eliminates cold and fatigue, supports the bones by strengthening marrow, improves appetite and increases lactation in breast-feeding mothers. Too much chicken causes wind and if chicken is eaten during a cold or fever, it will make the symptoms worse.

When combined with black beans, chicken's energy and blood-building qualities make it a good tonic after childbirth or for people who have had chronic illnesses.

Chicken liver nurtures the qi, blood, liver and kidneys, and removes blood stagnation and cold. It may be used to treat blurred vision, impotence, incontinence and childhood malnutrition.

Chinese red dates are also known as jujubes and are sweet and warm. They are a great pick-me-up if you feel weak and irritable. They replenish the stomach, spleen and blood and act as a sedative, so that you can relax and let the body restore itself. Specifically, Chinese dates should ease diarrhoea, poor appetite, anaemia and heart palpitations. However they should be avoided if you have bleeding gums.

Many Chinese women eat jujubes everyday because of legends that claim the fruit has special longevity powers and makes people look much younger than their years.

Chives add both taste and warmth to a meal without being too heating, so they are perfect for use by almost everyone. Like many herbs, the warmth of chives helps the digestive system by providing extra warmth for the process. Specifically, chives increase balance in the stomach and help ease distension, nausea and vomiting caused by cold in the body. Chives are also good for treating blood stagnation generally and in the blood vessels around the heart, so they can be helpful with chest pain or clearing bruising after an injury. Chives dry damp and improve qi circulation.

Chrysanthemum flowers in tea, clear heat in the liver, remove toxins, counteract blurry vision and brighten the eyes. Pungent, sweet, bitter and cool, they can treat a cold, headaches, blood-shot eyes, hypertension and urinary tract infections, particularly if the tongue is red with a yellow coating. Chrysanthemum tea with honey can be helpful if you have a sore throat. Avoid commercially grown chrysanthemums as they will have been sprayed with chemicals.

Cinnamon is sweet and warm and can become a powerful friend to anyone feeling weak, chilled, or hot and cold at the same time. The kidneys are considered the gate to the fire of life. Cinnamon stokes this fire, eliminates chill, eases diarrhoea and pain in the lower back and knees, improves circulation to warm cold hands and feet and provides energy balance to people who are feeling hot in the upper part of the body and cold in the lower half.

Clams are cold, salty and sinking. They tone yin, clear heat, moisturise dryness, remove damp and phlegm and strengthen the liver and kidneys. Clams can be used to treat swelling, vaginal discharge, dry coughs, night sweats and haemorrhoids.

Cloves are warm and descending. This means they warm the kidney and genital area and can be helpful to women who are infertile because of cold in the uterus, or to men with empty yang impotence. While there are many reasons for both infertility and impotence, in both these cases, strengthening the yang is very important and gentle warming foods, such as cloves, provide that boost to yang. They push the yang down to the reproductive organs where it is needed, without moving so fast that yin is harmed in the process. Cloves are also useful to relieve other cold-related symptoms such as hiccuping, abdominal pain and excessive, clear vaginal discharge.

Coconut is sweet and strengthening and builds yin. It clears wind and summer heat and counteracts weakness, dampness and nosebleed. Coconut milk is best used by people who don't consume much fat in the rest of their diet.

Coriander pushes up and out once it is inside the body. It encourages sweating, and removes stagnation of the blood. Although measles are no longer common, coriander is useful for anyone experiencing a long incubation period of measles, but it shouldn't be eaten by anyone who is already experiencing an outbreak.

Early English traders called coriander 'Chinese parsley', and the Chinese term for parsley can be translated as 'foreign coriander'.

Corn provides strength and opens and relaxes the heart, so it is particularly good for people with heart disease. Anyone suffering hypertension, gallstones or jaundice will benefit from adding corn to their diet. Corn also regulates digestion, keeps the teeth and gums healthy and strengthens the kidneys.

Crab promotes the healing of broken bones. It can treat scabies and some forms of dermatitis. Crab should not be eaten too regularly as it is very cold in nature and is also considered toxic when over-consumed.

Crayfish is warm, unlike crab. It acts as a supplement for the kidneys, which contain our life force. Including crayfish in a meal or two can be a strengthening tonic for anyone recovering from a stroke.

Cucumber is a cooling addition to a summertime meal. Cucumber clears heat, toxins and inflammation from the body. Its cool, descending nature makes it perfect to treat conditions that occur in the upper body, including mental depression, sore throat and conjunctivitis. Cucumbers quench thirst and soothe irritability. On the other hand, cucumber can exacerbate lower body symptoms, such as abdominal pain or diarrhoea.

Daikon or white radish, is pungent, sweet and cool. In the lungs, it eases raspy coughs, asthma and laryngitis. In the stomach, it promotes digestion.

Dandelion is sweet, bitter and cold. It removes heat and toxins in the blood and clears dampness. Dandelion can be used to treat jaundice, boils or urinary tract infections.

> When gathering or using herbs, take the part of the plant that correlates with the current season – in spring, use the leaves; in summer, the flowers; in autumn, the twigs; and in winter, the roots.

Dang gui is a Chinese herb that can be used in cooking to overcome weakness. It is also known as tang-kuei or Chinese angelica root – not to be confused with European angelica. Dang gui is sweet, pungent and warm and its main claim to fame is its ability to nourish the blood and invigorate circulation. While it is not recommended for anyone with diarrhoea, small amounts of dang gui added to soup can provide strength for people with a weak heart, arthritis, anaemia, menstrual problems or for people who have had a traumatic injury. Avoid dang gui if bleeding heavily.

Dill counteracts many of the toxins found in meat and fish, so it can be very helpful to anyone with a sensitive stomach. It promotes appetite and can be used to treat anorexia.

Duck is cool and an antidote for dryness and heat within the body. It also reduces swelling.

Eel can help us deal with wind inside the body (in spring) and can ease ailments such as arthritis and colds which are caused by exposure to wind. Eel's effect on the kidneys is to strengthen the bones. Its effect on the liver is to strengthen the sinews. A meal of eel may also help with haemorrhoids and post-partum loss of bladder control.

Eggplant is particularly good for the blood as it both cools the blood and gets it moving. It can counteract problems caused by eating too much meat and it helps move stagnation, especially in the liver. Swellings or sores can be relieved by eating eggplant, as can clotting during menstruation. Eggplant may also stop imbalanced flow such as diarrhoea.

Eggs are yin and benefit all five zang organs – the heart, lungs, spleen, kidneys and liver. Eggs are highly nutritious and counter dryness. They brighten eyes, clear blurred vision and conjunctivitis and soothe a dry throat and cough or a hoarse voice. The ascending energy of eggs makes them helpful to treat diarrhoea and to calm a restless foetus. This same ascending energy can cause nausea in some people, or contribute to wind symptoms such as dizziness and nervousness.

> For people who don't like to consume many dairy products, one way to improve your calcium intake is to occasionally mix very finely ground eggshells into your food.

Endive   is a type of lettuce with a very bitter flavour, which in TCM is the flavour connected to the heart. In Britain during the 1600s, Culpepper said, 'Endive is available for the fainting, swooning and passions of the heart. It cannot be used amiss.'

Fennel   is pungent and warm and can rid you of flatulence. It relieves pain by expelling cold and easing distension and regulates the flow of qi. For some men, fennel can relieve pain in the testes.

Figs   create fluid in the body, so they can treat a dry, sore throat or a dry cough. They can also rectify constipation. They strengthen the spleen, ease indigestion and clear blockages in the abdomen and intestines. Figs may be helpful to control skin eruptions and boils.

> Of garlic, Culpepper said, '… in men oppressed by melancholy it will … send up … many strange visions to the head: therefore, inwardly, let it be taken with great moderation.'

Garlic   is warming, removes cold from the body and gives sluggish qi a boost. It destroys worms and treats malaria, tuberculosis, pneumonia, snake bite and hepatitis – a powerful food. A little bit can go a long way. Because of its ascending, warming nature, it is better to avoid garlic if you have problems with your throat or head, such as toothache or conjunctivitis, or signs of heat such as a red face or a red tongue with a yellow coating.

Ginger can be warm or hot. Dried ginger is hot, so it can be added to a dish when you need a considerable warming effect, such as warming cold hands and feet. It has a calming effect and warms the spleen and stomach, which can help with morning sickness or chronic vomiting. Fresh ginger is warm rather than hot. It helps remove phlegm, stagnation and cold, which means it can be helpful if you have a cold, phlegmy cough (with white, rather than yellow, phlegm), or rheumatism. When you have a yellow tongue (indicating heat) it is better to avoid ginger.

> In 1597, John Gerard said of ginger, 'it is of a heating and digesting qualitie, and is profitable for the stomacke.'

Ginkgo biloba or bai guo is a sweet and bitter herb that can be added to soups to help people with a persistent cough or asthma. Only add one of two small pieces to soup and avoid if you have symptoms of cold or dampness. Check your tongue!

Goose helps all the organs work together well in winter.

Grapes are autumn's strength and energy capsules. They strengthen tendons and bones, nourish the blood, ease coughs caused by weakness in the lungs and can be used to help to relieve symptoms of night sweats, rheumatism, swelling, anaemia or excessive appetite. Avoid grapes if your tongue coating is white and sticky.

Grapefruit is cooling. If you have a hangover, use grapefruit as part of your recovery plan as it helps push down the rebellious qi that is moving up after drinking too much (because of the heat and sweet effects of alcohol). That same downward motion of grapefruit can help ease burping and indigestion. The cooling effect of grapefruits mean they also help reduce fevers and eliminate toxins.

Green beans or string beans are particularly good for the spleen and kidneys. Strengthening the kidneys may help stop middle of the night trips to the toilet, while supporting the spleen can help stop white vaginal discharge.

Hawthorn fruit or shan zha is sour, sweet and slightly warm. It improves digestion and invigorates blood circulation to help remove stagnant fatty food from the digestive system and ease any sense of abdominal fullness and associated pain. Hawthorn fruit is also helpful to counteract hypertension.

Hazelnuts are an antidote for weakness and will brighten your eyes, but, as with any nut, only eat a few lightly cooked a couple of times a week. Hazelnuts are especially good for anyone who is emaciated or suffering from malnutrition or has chronic diarrhoea.

Honey is warm and moistening, so it gets things moving along. Constipation, stomach-ache, sinusitis and tension are all blockages that will benefit from a spoonful of honey. Honey is the last thing to eat if you have diarrhoea. The pure sweetness of honey helps to get rid of toxins both inside and outside the body, so if you have a sore throat, honey will moisten the dryness and fight the germs. Add half a tablespoon to a cup of warm water, stir and drink. While processed honey can add to dampness within the body, raw honey clears damp and, in moderation, is useful to treat water retention or excess weight, as long as there are no heat symptoms such as a yellow tongue. Raw honey will also speed up recovery from a hangover and help people with an alcohol dependence.

Job's tears barley is an excellent spleen support. As it strengthens, barley also clears and helps ease inflammation and remove damp and pus from the body. It's good to eat a warm barley soup if you have rheumatic arthritis, a skin infection, acne, tinea of the foot, swelling or an infected wound.

Kelp is cooling and salty. It increases yin fluids, softens hardness, removes phlegm, strengthens the kidneys and removes toxins. As long as your stomach and spleen are in good shape, kelp is very useful for getting rid of heat from the body and alleviating dryness. Kelp can also be used to treat arthritis, high blood pressure, swelling, anaemia and problems with swallowing. Kelp's cooling properties soothe the lungs and throat, ease asthma, help with weight loss and rejuvenate tired muscles.

Kidney beans are sweet, act as a diuretic and remove damp and swelling, while also building yin fluids. They are good for the heart and the kidneys.

Kohlrabi is a mixture of pungent, sweet and bitter, so its flavours benefit the lungs, spleen and heart. Kohlrabi dries damp, removes stagnant blood, expels cold and assists yang and qi. It can also help you sober up.

Lamb is warming, but clears excessive heat. It warms the digestive system and sends warmth down to the lower body. It can be particularly beneficial for the legs, liver and kidneys which are likely to suffer from cold complaints, especially in winter. Some wintertime abdominal pain is caused by letting this area get too cold (internally and externally) so lamb soup is a useful remedy. After childbirth, many women are susceptible to cold in the lower half of their bodies so lamb broth can be beneficial and comforting. Lamb improves qi, blood production and lactation and can be used to treat anaemia, weakness and some cases of impotence.

Lamb kidney is a great tonic for the kidneys. And since the kidneys are the gate of life and are rarely too strong, you can benefit from eating lamb kidneys any time of year. Problems associated with the kidneys include fatigue, lower back pain, weak legs and knees, deafness, excessive urination, incontinence, impotence and premature ejaculation, which can all be assisted by eating lamb kidneys.

Leek is pungent and a gentle warmer. Leek treats diarrhoea, removes excess heat from the stomach and can ease bleeding gums. For people with signs of heat or excess, leek is an excellent substitute for onion.

Lemons are sour and astringent and strengthen the liver. They clear phlegm but create moisture, so they are a good treatment for coughs with a dry, sore throat. Lemons freshen breath as they clear bacteria in both the mouth and the intestines. Lemon juice, diluted with warm water, can be useful for damp heat problems such as bladder infections.

Lentils benefit the heart, improve circulation and help build the jing of the kidneys. They improve the health and appearance of the hair and facial complexion and strengthen willpower and enhance our ability to be content.

Lettuce naturally dries dampness in the body so it is excellent for people wanting to lose weight. Generally, fat is made up of dampness and phlegm and is aggravated by cold and raw foods. While anyone who is chronically overweight should stick predominantly to warm, cooked meals that are easy on the digestive system, lettuce is an exception. It also clears heat in the body, which shows on the tongue as red with a yellow coating. Lettuce is also good for breast-feeding mothers as it encourages lactation. However, too much lettuce can cause dizziness.

> The bitter flavour and heat-reducing properties of lettuce identified in TCM may explain the soporific effect noted by Beatrix Potter in *The Tale of the Flopsy Bunnies*.

Lychees regulate the qi and have descending energy, which makes them useful to stop hiccups. They benefit the heart and spleen which means they can ease insomnia, nervous excitement and anxiety. Lychees can also ease toothache.

Longan supports the spleen, nourishes the heart and grounds the spirit, which eases heart palpitations, insomnia, restlessness, poor memory and nervousness.

Lotus root is cold and descending and quickly cools the blood. It also tones the spleen and blood and helps produce muscles. Cooked, lotus root can be beneficial to people suffering from anorexia. If you feel you are being strangled by the heat and are so thirsty that drinking water isn't enough, the answer may well be fresh lotus root.

Lotus seeds nourish the heart and quiet the spirit. They help ease and calm dreams that disturb sleep and they lessen heart palpitations, insomnia and restlessness. Lotus seeds also support the kidneys, stopping spontaneous seminal emissions, and the spleen, treating diarrhoea and poor appetite.

Mandarin peel is pungent, bitter and warm. By getting rid of flatulence from the digestive system, mandarin peel tones the vital energy of the spleen. It also removes dampness and phlegm, and reverses the rebellious upward flow of qi, to ease abdominal distension, phlegmy coughs, hiccups and vomiting.

Millet is cool, sweet and salty, with a descending energy. It balances the stomach and spleen, builds yin fluids, supports the kidneys and counteracts toxins in the body. It can help ease indigestion, vomiting, stomach heat, diarrhoea, diabetes and morning sickness. Millet also sweetens the breath. However, if you have weak digestion and chronic watery stools, choose a gentler grain such as rice.

Mulberries are cool and sweet and benefit the kidneys, blood and the liver. They may be helpful for people with ringing in the ears or dizziness, blurred vision and night blindness. They can also be beneficial to people who have joint pain, anaemia, insomnia and premature greying of the hair.

Approximately 50 per cent of 50-year-olds already have 50 per cent grey hair. According to TCM, grey hair is connected to your internal organs and affected by diet. Pass those mulberries!

Mung beans are sweet and cool. They are excellent for summer. They clear heat, tone yin, counteract toxins and cool and calm the liver. The downward energy of mung beans can be used to treat mumps, conjunctivitis, high blood pressure, diarrhoea and swelling. Mung bean sprouts are cold and can be used to treat alcoholism, but should be avoided if there are signs of cold in the body.

Mushrooms are terrific both in spring and autumn and benefit the stomach and lungs and calm the spirit. Specifically, mushrooms remove phlegm and toxins. They also relieve fatigue and boost energy. If you have a phlegmy cough, mushrooms may help but they can be difficult to digest. (See also SHIITAKE MUSHROOMS)

Musk melons clear heat from the body. They may relieve mild depression.

Mussels are warm and salty in nature which means they can be very useful to draw energy inwards, so they can be a good antidote for night sweats. The organs mussels affect most are the liver and kidneys. They can strengthen tendons and ease some cases of impotence, as well as treating lumbago, vertigo, intestinal blockage and abdominal swelling. Mussels also improve the qi and jing essence and build blood.

Mustard greens improve qi and circulation and are good for the lungs, which they expand and clear. So if you have a heavy feeling in the chest, are panting or coughing up white phlegm, a meal with mustard greens is likely to help. However, if you are coughing up yellow phlegm or have inflamed eyes, mustard greens will be too heating, and should be avoided.

Mustard seeds are pungent and warm. They get the circulation going which helps clear lumps from the body and ease pain and numbness in the joints. Mustard seeds also warm the lungs and remove phlegm.

Nutmeg is pungent and strengthens the qi. Inside the body, it warms and clears and is particularly beneficial for the intestines. Nutmeg treats vomiting and abdominal distension. Long-term and early morning diarrhoea can often be helped by adding nutmeg to stews and soups.

Oats are sweet and slightly bitter. They strengthen the spleen and boost energy. Warm oat porridge is an excellent booster for anyone who wants to feel stronger and calmer. Oats also strengthen heart muscles, balance fluids in the body and can decrease perspiration that isn't linked to exertion.

Olives are good for the throat and lungs. They produce fluids, counteract toxins and act as an astringent in the body. They can also assist with a hangover, dry cough, sore throat or chronic diarrhoea.

Onions are pungent and sweet and they get the qi and blood moving. They can be used to treat blockages, such as damp, bruises and swellings; cold and toxins, such as headaches; hardening of the arteries; nasal congestion and worms. Like garlic, onions are a very strong food and eating too many of them fosters excessive emotional desires that make us demanding and needy. (see also SHALLOTS and SPRING ONIONS)

Oranges are sweet, sour and cool. They quench thirst and moisten the lungs, letting the qi flow freely in the chest and easing coughs. Oranges are useful to treat vomiting and poor appetite.

Boil orange peel for half an hour, allow to cool. Then drink the liquid as a hangover cure.

Orange peel is sour, bitter and warm. While it is not something you'll eat everyday, it can be a very useful ingredient for both taste and health. It dries dampness, gets rid of phlegm, and eases indigestion, hiccups, burping, vomiting, a heavy chest and a poor appetite.

Oregano helps clear the body of undigested food that can cause bad breath. It also improves appetite and clears heat, swelling and dampness.

Oysters are sweet and salty and are good for the liver and kidneys. They tone the yin and nourish the blood. They can help with insomnia, nervousness, indecision and restlessness. Oysters tone qi and moisten dryness. Oysters, and other foods that support yin, encourage you to be more practical and grounded. But oysters shouldn't be eaten by anyone with a skin problem, such as a rash, as they encourage the body's energy to move up and out which only exacerbates an existing skin problem. They may also be too nourishing for people with excessive damp in their bodies.

Papaya is cold, but it supports the spleen and stomach and improves digestion. It also clears heat, stops coughing, eases rheumatism, alleviates thirst, dries damp, eases difficult defecation and promotes urination.

Parsley is pungent, bitter, salty and warm. It supports the kidneys, aids digestion and removes toxins, especially from meat. Parsley also removes mucus that causes swelling and distension. It can be useful for people with high blood pressure.

Peaches encourage the body to produce more fluid and moisten the intestines. People with a hot or dry cough or heat rising will find peaches helpful.

Peanut oil pushes downwards and helps get rid of accumulations from the digestive process and may ease conjunctivitis.

Peanuts moisten and strengthen the lungs and ease indigestion, however, they should be avoided if you have any cold or damp problems. They can be used to treat dry coughs. Peanuts are often served at the beginning of a banquet to stimulate appetite. Fried peanuts boost yang and increase heat. Boiled peanuts relieve damp and swelling.

Pears are the dietary answer to the dryness many people experience in the lungs during autumn. They help the body, especially the lungs, produce fluids while getting rid of phlegm. Pears clear heat and tone the qi and blood. Avoid pears if you have a weak digestive system. Alternatively, cook them.

Peas are sweet and they enhance digestion, strengthen the spleen and stomach and protect it from the effects of an overheated liver. When stomach qi is rebelling (moving up instead of down) and causing vomiting, hiccups or burping, peas can send the qi down again. Peas may also help with skin eruptions and constipation.

Pepper is pungent and warming for the stomach and spleen. It helps ease cold-induced vomiting, diarrhoea, abdominal pain and the effects of food poisoning. (See also BLACK PEPPER)

Black pepper is the immature fruit of *Piper nigrum*; white pepper is the dried mature fruit after processing.

Peppermint is a pungent, cooling herb. Summer colds with fever, headache, sore throat and red eyes will benefit from peppermint. Premenstrual grumpiness and breast and abdominal pain may be alleviated too as peppermint helps move liver stagnation. Heat-related pain that is eased by peppermint includes migraines and headaches, sore throats, indigestion and toothache.

Persimmons moisten the lungs and can assist with high blood pressure, coughs, sores in the mouth and hiccups. The coughing and wheezing of asthma can often be eased by introducing persimmons to the diet. But eating persimmons is not a good idea if you have diarrhoea – unless the persimmon in question is not yet ripe, in which case it can help diarrhoea.

Pineapple is a good option in summer if you are suffering from insomnia. It can also help if you have low blood pressure or don't have enough strength in your hands and feet. However it is important to make sure the fruit is fully ripe as unripe fruit can cause stomach cramps and damage teeth.

Pine nuts are sweet and can help sufferers of rheumatism and dizziness as they open the energy paths inside our bodies and remove wind. Pine nuts provide moisture for the lungs which can ease a dry cough, and for the intestines which eases constipation.

It is best to shell nuts and seeds right before eating or cooking as they tend to go rancid without the natural protection of skin or shell.

Pistachios are bitter and sweet. They support the liver and kidneys and improve the appearance of the eyes and hair. Pistachios also moisten the intestines which eases constipation.

Plums predominantly affect the liver and kidneys. Their heat-clearing properties mean they calm the liver, which can have a positive affect on anger levels and nervous disorders (especially purple plum varieties). They also help with indigestion, bleeding gums and sores on the tongue and in the mouth. (See also UMEBOSI PLUMS)

Pomegranate is sweet, sour, astringent and cool. It eases diarrhoea, coughs, sore throats and mouth ulcers. It can also help to strengthen gums and expel worms such as tapeworms from the large intestine.

Pork is sweet and a little bitter. In small amounts, pork is an excellent antidote for weakness as it supplements the blood and yin. It also supports the kidneys which are the gate of life. Pork is very nutritious and moistens the body, so it can ease a dry cough or dry constipation. New mothers will get their strength back more quickly if they eat a little pork.

Pork kidney is like a double booster for our own kidneys since all pork supports the kidneys, and eating kidneys from any animal is one of the best kidney tonics available. Pork kidney can help with lower back pain, night sweats and deafness caused by aging. Pork kidney also strengthens the bladder so, with exercises, may be useful for women who have lost a degree of bladder control after child-birth.

Potatoes strengthen kidney yin and are considered a staple in many cultures. Potatoes help with most deficiencies and are particularly good for the spleen and qi. Their reputation as a comfort food is well deserved. Potatoes heal inflammation, so they are good for people with mumps, stomach ulcers, rheumatism, laryngitis and tonsillitis. For people with these conditions, fried potatoes should be avoided.

Prawns get the body going and encourage qi to move up and out. They are good for qi, blood, yang, liver and kidneys. They are also good for breast-feeding mothers as they promote lactation. Their ascending nature means they also push cold, phlegm, wind, worms and stagnation out of the body. However, if you are still weak after illness, they can be too much of a good thing – stick to gentler tonics for a while. Prawns treat some cases of impotence, but avoid them if you have any form of skin rash or problems with premature ejaculation because they will make the problem worse.

Pumpkin counteracts toxins and is damp. However, if there is too much damp in the body – indicated by a heavy, sticky coating on the tongue – it is best avoided, especially if it has been steamed.

Pumpkin seeds are good for breast-feeding mothers. They are also particularly good for helping to get rid of worms as they act as a relaxant so worms are easier to dislodge (especially roundworm and tapeworms).

Radishes are cool and clear heat, but also remove cold from the body. Radishes clear undigested bits of food from our systems and may help relieve distension, phlegmy coughs, and migraine headaches.

Raspberries tone the liver, kidneys and blood, brighten the eyes and slow down the greying of hair. They can help with impotence, sterility, fatigue, blurred vision and too frequent urination. Raspberries regulate menstruation and treat anaemia. On the other hand, you should avoid raspberries if you are experiencing difficulty urinating.

Rhubarb is bitter and cold. It is usually the root that is used in herbal remedies, while the stems make a delicious dessert. Rhubarb acts as a purgative, removes heat and stagnation, improves circulation and treats jaundice. It can be used to ease fever with constipation and to remove stomach blockages.

Rice is sweet, gentle and supportive to the spleen and stomach. It replenishes their vital energy. If you feel less than perfect, rice is an excellent base for any meal – perhaps it is the original comfort food. Rice helps to relieve thirst and diarrhoea and can ease mental depression. Brown rice has more nutrients than white rice but is also harder to digest, so you may need to stick to white rice if brown rice is too much for your system. Alternatively, before cooking, soak brown rice in water overnight.

Long-grain rice is better for summer, and short-grain rice is better suited to the colder months. Basmati rice is lighter than other rice varieties, so is best for people with damp conditions, or for people trying to lose weight.

Rosemary can treat menstrual pain and may delay premature balding.

Rye is bitter. It dries damp, so it is a good substitute for wheat if you are overweight, or have a constantly runny nose when there are no other symptoms of a cold. Rye also affects the liver, removing stagnation, so can be used to treat migraines as well as moodiness that swings from angry outbursts to depression. Rye cooked as sourdough bread (and therefore more sour) is even better for the liver.

Saffron gets the blood and qi moving and removes blockages, especially in the liver. It is useful for women whose periods have stopped (amenorrhoea), or women who have painful periods, or have abdominal pain or dizziness after giving birth. Saffron is also helpful with heart and chest pain and injuries from impacts such as falling or being hit. This same ability to get things moving means that saffron should not be eaten by anyone who is pregnant.

Sardines strengthen the bones and tendons. They get the blood moving, tone yin, warm the spleen and stomach, promote good circulation and boost energy.

Seaweed is cold and bitter and sinks because of its salty nature. Seaweed clears heat, counteracts dryness and tones yin. It is used to ease chronic bronchitis, hypertension and abdominal swelling and obstruction. The salty flavour tends to soften hardness and it can be useful in the treatment of lumps, goiter and scrofula. Seaweed should be used sparingly by people with a spleen deficiency and signs of damp.

Sesame supports the liver and kidneys specifically, but is good for the heart, lungs and spleen, too. It helps with dizziness, vertigo and premature greying of the hair. Sesame is particularly good for breast-feeding mothers, especially for those who aren't producing enough milk. It may also help counteract vertigo and rheumatism. (See also BLACK SESAME)

Sesame oil is cooling and moisturises both the skin and internal systems so it encourages bowel movements, eases some abdominal pain, and soothes dry skin and skin irritations.

Shallots are warm, pungent and bitter. They remove cold, but also clear heat, which can ease a common cold that is accompanied by fever, chills and a headache. Shallots dry damp and expand the chest, so can help with chest pain, heart pain, dry retching and skin eruptions. (see also ONIONS and SPRING ONIONS)

Shark or flake, tones all the zang organs – heart, lungs, spleen, liver and kidneys – boosts qi and reduces swelling.

Shiitake mushrooms are sweet and are used to treat coughs, prevent hardening of the arteries and soothe reactions to food toxins that may be present in meat. (See also MUSHROOMS)

Soybean oil is hot and sedates yin. It lubricates the intestines, can help with constipation and can expel worms from the body.

Soybeans are cool, sweet and descending. They clear heat and strengthen the spleen and kidneys. Soybeans relax the intestines, which can ease some abdominal pains and treat distension. Soybeans cleanse blood vessels and the heart, so are excellent for people with red faces and strong constitutions. They should ease conjunctivitis and may be used to treat alcoholism. (See also BLACK SOYBEANS)

Spearmint is pungent and warm and counteracts the affects of cold and wind as it supports the qi and blood and gets them moving. Spearmint has a pain-numbing effect, so it is useful if you have a cold, headache or menstrual pain.

Spelt is warm and sweet and strengthens the spleen and nurtures yin. It originated in South-East Asia and is a type of wheat. Spelt, along with kamut, doesn't tend to produce allergies the way wheat does, so can be useful as an alternative to wheat. Because of its yin-building qualities, it is a great strengthener for people with chronic weakness, such as arthritis.

Spinach	is cool and sweet and slippery. Its descending energy and slippery form make it an excellent antidote for constipation. Spinach also has an astringent effect on yin and it nourishes the blood while it actually helps to stop bleeding – so it is good for anyone who suffers regular nose bleeds.
Spring onions	are pungent and bitter. They can clear toxins from meat, strengthen the nervous system, remove damp, ease pain and clear the mind. Spring onions also help relieve cold symptoms such as cold stomach-ache. (see also ONIONS and SHALLOTS)
Squid	is particularly good for the liver and kidneys. It improves the health of the reproduction system, including easing blocked menstruation.
Star anise	is pungent, sweet and warm. It dispels cold from the abdomen and regulates the circulation of the qi to strengthen the body. Star anise has an anti-fungal and anti-bacterial effect so is good for anyone fighting infection.
Strawberries	expel cold, tone the liver and kidneys and act as an astringent in the body. They are excellent for removing damp. In summer, when they are in season, the occasional bowl of these sweet fruits should be considered a part of any weight-loss program. Strawberries can help you get over general feelings of weakness, a lack of appetite, dizziness, vertigo or a hangover.

In ancient Europe, women used crushed strawberries to whiten their complexions.

Sweet potato benefits all the organs, but especially the spleen and kidneys. It supports the qi and blood while removing cold and stagnancy. Sweet potato balances the intestines, so it can treat both diarrhoea and constipation. And sweet potato can help men guard against premature ejaculation.

Tangerines clear heat, quench thirst and moisten the lungs. Heat is, in general, more likely to be an issue in the upper part of the body. Tangerines moisten the lungs and push energy downwards in the body, which means they can treat chest congestion, vomiting, hiccups and diabetes.

Better to be without food for three days, than without tea for one.
– Ancient Chinese saying.

Tea made from young tea leaves is diuretic, anti-toxic and anti-bacterial. Too much green tea can give some people heart palpitations.

Black tea is warm and strengthens the stomach.

Green tea is cool and bitter and affects the heart. Green tea reduces fever, clears phlegm, heat and flatulence, aids digestion, promotes the production of body fluid, quenches thirst, brightens the eyes, calms and refreshes the mind, improves the memory and regulates the function of the lungs and stomach.

Green tea is good for the young and strong. As you get older, choose a Chinese black tea such as Puerh.

Thyme should ease complaints caused by wind, such as hot-type coughs, abdominal distension, indigestion or a common cold accompanied by a headache, cough, aches and pains and a sore throat.

Tomatoes are sweet and sour. They promote appetite and digestion, strengthen the stomach, moisten dryness, calm the liver and clear heat. The descending energy of tomatoes enables them to ease high blood pressure, mouth sores, dizziness and red eyes as excess heat is moved down and out of the body. Too many tomatoes can weaken the digestive system and cause damp.

Trout is hot and sour. It pushes cold out and warms up the body (especially the stomach) which is good for digestion.

Tuna is a great energy food. It strengthens qi and removes damp, which is the biggest energy-sapper. This damp-removing quality means tuna is a good food if the weather is damp or if you are fatigued or have dampness blocking the body's energy pathways with damp conditions such as rheumatism.

Turnips are pungent, bitter and sweet. And, although turnips have often been considered fit only for pigs or peasants, they play an important role in our diets as they clear heat and remove dampness and phlegm. Damp and phlegm can block the efficient functioning of all the organs to some degree. They can also block smooth flow of qi around the body and cause obesity, depression and rheumatism. Foods that remove damp are essential to bring many people into balance.

Umebosi plums are surprisingly sour, and are a powerful astringent and 'tightener' for the lungs, intestines, liver and spleen. They help ease coughs, diarrhoea, bleeding and they also kill worms. (see also PLUMS)

Venison is sweet and warm and nourishes the liver and kidneys. It also strengthens the bones and the tendons and eases problems with knee and lower back pain, premature ejaculation, impotence and sterility.

Vinegar is sour, bitter and warm. It dries damp, stops bleeding, gets rid of toxins, removes stagnant blood, improves circulation and encourages perspiration.

Walnuts tone and warm both the lungs and the kidneys (specifically the kidney yang that relates to function), and moisturise the intestines. Walnuts calm the nerves and ease lower back and knee soreness. They nourish sperm and in some cases can fix impotence. They can also be used to treat anaemia. Walnuts are good for the lungs of asthmatics as they are both warming and calming, which helps ease coughing and wheezing. However, if you are coughing up yellow sputum, don't eat walnuts – you already have signs of heat and the walnuts could make things worse. Walnuts can be hard on digestion, so eat only one a day to support the kidneys and lungs without harming the spleen.

> The botanical name for walnuts is *Juglans regia*, which refers to the early nickname, Jupiter's nut – it was thought that when the gods roamed on the Earth, they lived on walnuts.

Water chestnuts have a cold, descending energy that clears heat and removes phlegm and build-up in the body, including distension. They ease blood pressure, soothe red, painful eyes or conjunctivitis, and are good for diabetics.

Watercress is pungent, bitter, sweet and cooling. Watercress strengthens qi and builds blood and yin. The moistening quality of watercress affects the lungs, stomach, liver and bladder. It relieves a dry, sore throat, a cough with yellow phlegm (which indicates heat in the lungs), restlessness and grumpiness.

Watermelon is sweet and cold and benefits the bladder and spleen. It encourages urination and clears heat and eases sores in the mouth, thirst and mental depression. And it is another remedy for a hangover. Watermelon is best eaten on a hot day when the sun is out. However if your tongue is white, showing signs of cold, or damp cold, only have a small amount of watermelon.

Wheat is cool, sweet, calming and strengthening. It nourishes the heart and shen, supports the kidneys, and clears swelling. Wheat brings energy down into the lower half of the body – otherwise that energy might cause heat and worry in the head. Wheat can ease insomnia, palpitations, irritability and night sweats. One of wheat's advantages is that it encourages growth, which is also why people trying to lose weight may wish to restrict their intake.

Wheat germ is cold and pungent and tones yin, especially of the heart and kidneys. It strengthens the qi, and treats mental depression.

Wolfberry fruit is available in Chinese stores as gou qi zi or lycium fruit. It replenishes liver and kidney yin, which houses our vital essence. It nourishes blood, improves eyesight, eases aching back and legs and helps with impotence and vertigo. However, wolfberry fruit is too hard on the spleen for anyone with spleen dampness or diarrhoea.

Yams tone the spleen, lungs and kidneys. Yams treat deficiency in the spleen qi which can otherwise lead to loose stools, diarrhoea and white vaginal discharge.

Yoghurt is sweet, sour and warm. It provides moisture for the lungs and intestines to relieve dry coughs, thirst, agitation and dry constipation.

Glossary of basic terms

Essence – our life force, known as jing.

Fu – five yang organs that deal with food transportation: stomach, small intestine, gallbladder, large intestine and bladder.

Jing – life force or essence, which is stored in the major organs, but predominantly in the kidneys.

Nei Jing – one of the oldest surviving texts on traditional Chinese medicine. Also called The Yellow Emperor's Classic of Internal Medicine.

Pillars – the four pillars, exercise, diet, rest and mental balance, provide support for the treasures of essence, energy and spirit.

Qi – (pronounced chee) energy flows within the body.

Righteous qi – energy flows within the body moving in the appropriate patterns.

Rebellious qi – energy flows within the body moving against the appropriate patterns.

Shen – the spirit-mind, which resides in the heart.

TCM – traditional Chinese medicine.

Treasures – there are three treasures: essence or jing, energy or qi, and the spirit-mind called shen.

Wei qi – the body's immune system, which is ruled by the lungs.

Yang – typically action, hot, male, upper, back, acute, opposite of yin.

Yin – typically substance, cold, female, lower, front, chronic, opposite of yang.

Zang – the five major organs, which are yin and include the heart, lungs, spleen, liver and kidneys.

Glossary of food

Adzuki beans – small red beans, slightly bigger than lentils.

Chervil – herb belonging to the parsley family.

Kohlrabi – similar in size to a turnip, kohlrabi has purple skin, white flesh and little roots coming out of the skin that should be removed before cooking.

Kombu (seaweed) – type of dark sea kelp used to flavour long cooking soups or stews.

Longan – small, round, light, fleshy coloured fruit, often used dry. Similar to lychee but smaller.

Loquat – common in China and Japan, this small yellow fruit is about plum size.

Mustard greens – a large, dark leafy form of Chinese cabbage with a peppery taste.

Pak choy – is a smaller and lighter green version of the more common bok choy.

Shoyu – naturally fermented soy sauce made from wheat and soybeans.

Tamari – naturally fermented soy sauce made from soybeans. It is wheat-free.

Tempeh – fermented soybeans. Commonly used in Indonesian cooking, tempeh comes in a slab to be sliced like salami.

Turtle beans – originating in Mexico, they are often referred to as black beans in American cuisine. They require soaking for several hours and a long cooking time.

Wakame (seaweed) – a type of seaweed that should be briefly soaked in water.

Chinese herbs

These herbs are available at TCM dispensaries.

Bai guo (ginkgo biloba)

Dang gui (Chinese angelica root)

Dang shen (pilose asiabell root)

Da zao (Chinese red dates, jujubes)

Gou qi zi (wolfberry)

He shou wu (fleeceflower root)

Huang qi (astragalus root)

Rou cong rong (cistanche)

Shan yao (Chinese yam)

Shan zha (hawthorn fruit)

Tian ma (gastrodia tuber)

Conversion table

Millilitres	Fluid ounces	
5 ml		1 teaspoon
10 ml		2 teaspoons
15 ml	$^1/_2$ fl oz	
20 ml	$^2/_3$ fl oz	1 tablespoon
30ml	1 fl oz	
40 ml	$1^1/_3$ fl oz	
50 ml	$1^2/_3$ fl oz	
60 ml	2 fl oz	$^1/_4$ metric cup
75 ml	$2^1/_2$ fl oz	
80 ml	$2^3/_4$ fl oz	
90 ml	3 fl oz	
100 ml	$3^1/_2$fl oz	
125 ml	4 fl oz	$^1/_2$ metric cup
150 ml	5 fl oz	
200 ml	7 fl oz	
250 ml	8 fl oz	1 metric cup
300 ml	10 fl oz	
350 ml	12 fl oz	
400 ml	13 fl oz	
500 ml	16 fl oz	
750 ml	$1^1/_4$ pints	
1 litre	$1^2/_3$ pints	
2 litres	$3^1/_4$ pints	

Conversion table

Milligrams	Ounces
15 g	$^1/_2$ oz
20 g	$^2/_3$ oz
30 g	1 oz
40 g	$1^1/_3$ oz
50 g	$1^3/_4$ oz
60 g	2 oz
75 g	$2^2/_3$ oz
80 g	$2^3/_4$ oz
90 g	3 oz
100 g	$3^1/_2$ oz
125 g	4 oz
150 g	5 oz
200 g	7 oz
250 g	8 oz ($^1/_2$ lb)
300 g	$10^1/_2$ oz
350 g	$12^1/_3$ oz
400 g	14 oz
500 g	16 oz (1 lb)

Celsius	Fahrenheit
120°C	245°F
140°C	280°F
150°C	300°F
160°C	320°F
170°C	340°F
180°C	350°F
190°C	375°F
200°C	390°F
210°C	410°F
220°C	425°F
230°C	450°F

Bibliography

Stephanie Alexander
The Cook's Companion
Viking 1996
Melbourne

Sarah Brown
Vegetarian Cookbook
Doubleday 1984
Sydney

Allan Campion and Michele Curtis
Fresh
Purple Egg 2001
Melbourne

Jean Carper
The Food Pharmacy Guide to Good Eating
Bantam Books 1991
New York

Zhang Enqin (Ed)
Health Preservation and Rehabilitation
Publishing House of Shanghai
College of Traditional Chinese
Medicine 1988
Shanghai

Bob Flaws
The Tao of Healthy Eating
Blue Poppy Press 1998
Boulder, Colorado

Bob Flaws and Honora Wolfe
Prince Wen Hui's Cook
Paradigm Publications 1983
Brookline, Massachusetts

Dr Duo Gao (Ed)
The Encyclopedia of Chinese Medicine
HarperCollinsPublishers 1997
Sydney

Yin Huihe and Professor Shuai
Xuezhong
Fundamentals of Traditional Chinese
Medicine
Foreign Languages Press 1992
Beijing

Shi Lanhua, Zhang Enqin and
Wang Min
Basic Theory of Traditional Chinese
Medicine (Volumes 1 & 2)
Publishing House of Shanghai
College of Traditional Chinese
Medicine 1988
Shanghai

Henry C. Lu
Chinese System of Food Cures
Sterling Publishing Company 1986
New York

Penelope Ody
The Complete Medicinal Herbal
Viking 1993
Melbourne

Karen Phillipps and Martha Dahlen
A Popular Guide to Chinese Vegetables
MPH Bookstores 1985
Singapore

Bibliography

Paul Pitchford
Healing with Whole Foods
North Atlantic Books 1993
Berkeley, California

George Seddon
Your Vegetable Garden in Australia
Ure Smith Press 1978
Sydney

Ian Topliss *et al*. (Ed)
The Kitchen Diary 2002
Whiskbooks 2001
Melbourne

Wu Tsai-You
Chinese Food for Vigour and Beauty
Wu Juei Pao 1977
China

Bronwyn Whitlocke
Chinese Medicine for Women
Spinifex Press 1997
Melbourne

Xu Xiangcai and Zhang Wengao (Eds)
The English-Chinese Encyclopedia of Practical Traditional Chinese Medicine (9)
Higher Education Press 1989
Beijing

Him-che Yeung
Handbook of Chinese Herbs (2nd edition)
Institute of Chinese Medicine 1996
Rosemead, California

Zhou Zhao and George Ellis
The Healing Cuisine of China
Healing Arts Press 1998
Rochester, Vermont

Zhen Zhiya
Advanced Textbook on Traditional Chinese Medicine and Pharmacology
New World Press 1995
Beijing

Seasonal chart for a temperate climate

Early spring (September)

artichoke
asparagus
avocado
beans, broad
beetroot
bok choy
broccoli
cabbage
carrot
cauliflower
choy sum
cumquat
fennel

ginger
grapefruit
Jerusalem artichoke
leek
lemon
mandarin
mushroom
onion
orange
papaya
parsnip
pawpaw
pear

peas
pineapple
potato
pumpkin
rhubarb
rocket
silverbeet
sorrel
spinach
spring onion
tangelo
tarragon

Mid spring (October)

artichoke
asparagus
avocado
beans, broad & green
bok choy
broccoli
chervil
chives
cumquat
dill
garlic
grapefruit
Jerusalem artichoke
leek

lemon
loquat
mango
marjoram
onions
orange
oregano
papaya
parsnip
pawpaw
peas
pineapple
potato
raspberry

rhubarb
rocket
sage
sorrel
spring onion
strawberry
starfruit
silverbeet
spinach
tarragon
thyme
watercress

Late spring (November)

artichoke
asparagus
avocado
banana
beans, broad & green
beetroot
blueberry
celery
cherry
chervil
chives
coriander
cucumber
cumquat
dill
grapefruit

leek
lettuce
loquat
lychee
mango
marjoram
mint
onion
orange
oregano
papaya
pawpaw
peas
pineapple
potato
raspberry

rhubarb
rocket
sage
sorrel
spinach
spring onion
starfruit
strawberry
sweet corn
tarragon
thyme
tomato
watercress
zucchini flower

Early summer (December)

apricot
asparagus
avocado
banana
basil
beans, green & snake
blackberry
blueberry
capsicum
celery
cherry
chervil
chives
coriander
currants
cucumber
dill

eggplant
gooseberry
honeydew
lettuce
loganberry
lychee
mango
marjoram
mint
onion
orange
oregano
nectarine
passionfruit
pineapple
peach
peas

radish
raspberry
sage
spring onion
squash
starfruit
strawberry
sweet corn
thyme
tomato
watercress
watermelon
zucchini
zucchini flower

Mid summer (January)

apricot
avocado
banana
basil
beans, butter, green & snake
blackberry
blueberry
boysenberry
cantaloupe
capsicum
celery
cherry
chervil
chives
coriander
cucumber
currants

dill
eggplant
gooseberry
honeydew
lettuce
loganberry
lychee
marjoram
mulberry
mango
mint
nectarine
okra
onion
oregano
passionfruit
peach
peas

pineapple
plum
radish
raspberry
sage
spring onion
squash
starfruit
strawberry
sweet corn
tamarillo
thyme
tomato
watermelon
zucchini
zucchini flower

Late summer (February)

apple
avocado
banana
basil
beans, borlotti, butter, green & snake
blackberry
blueberry
boysenberry
cantaloupe
capsicum
celery

cherry
chilli
chives
coriander
cucumber
daikon
dill
eggplant
fig
grapes
guava
honeydew

kiwifruit
leek
lemon
lettuce
loganberry
lychee
mango
nectarine
okra
onion
orange
oregano

Late summer (February) continued

passionfruit
peach
pear
peas
plum
radish
thyme

tomato
raspberry
rhubarb
sage
spring onion
squash
starfruit

strawberry
sweet corn
tamarillo
tomato
watermelon
zucchini

Early autumn (March)

apple
almond
avocado
banana
basil
beans, borlotti, butter,
  green & snake
bok choy
breadfruit
cantaloupe
capsicum
celery
chestnut
chilli
choy sum
cucumber
daikon
eggplant
fig
grapes
guava

hazelnut
honeydew
kiwifruit
leek
lemon
lettuce
lime
mushroom
nectarine
pistachio
orange
papaya
passionfruit
peach
pear
persimmon
plum
pomegranate
rhubarb
tamarillo
okra

olive
onion
peas
potato
pumpkin
raspberry
shallots
silverbeet
spinach
spring onion
squash
strawberry
sweet corn
sweet potato
tarragon
tomato
walnut
watercress
zucchini

Mid autumn (April)

almond	garlic	peas
apple	ginger	persimmon
avocado	grapes	pistachio
banana	guava	plum
basil	hazelnut	pomegranate
beans, green & snake	honeydew	quince
beetroot	horseradish	potato
bok choy	kiwifruit	pumpkin
broccoli	leek	shallots
brussel sprouts	lemon	rhurbarb
cabbage	lettuce	silverbeet
capsicum	lime	spinach
carrot	mandarin	squash
cauliflower	mushroom	spring onion
celery	okra	sweet potato
chestnut	olive	swede
chilli	onions	tarragon
cucumber	orange	tomato
cumquat	papaya	turnip
daikon	parsnip	walnut
eggplant	passionfruit	watercress
fennel	peanut	zucchini
fig	pear	

Late autumn (May)

apple	brussel sprouts	chestnut
avocado	cabbage	cumquat
banana	carrot	custard apple
beetroot	cauliflower	daikon
bok choy	celeriac	fennel
broccoli	celery	garlic

Late autumn (May) continued

ginger
grapes
hazelnut
honeydew
horseradish
Jerusalem artichoke
kiwifruit
leek
lemon
lime
mandarin
mushroom
okra

olive
onions
orange
parsnip
peanut
pear
peas
persimmon
potato
pumpkin
quince
rhurbarb
shallots

silverbeet
spinach
squash
spring onion
swede
sweet potato
tarragon
tomato
turnip
walnut
watercress
witlof
zucchini

Early winter (June)

apples
avocado
bok choy
beetroot
broccoli
brussel sprouts
cabbage
carrot
cauliflower
celeriac
celery
chestnut
cumquat
custard apple
endive
fennel

garlic
ginger
hazelnut
horseradish
Jerusalem artichoke
kiwifruit
kohlrabi
leek
lemon
lime
mandarin
okra
olive
onion
orange
parsnip

passionfruit
pear
peas
persimmon
potato
pumpkin
quince
rhubarb
shallots
silverbeet
spinach
swede
sweet potato
turnip
walnut
witlof

Mid winter (July)

apples
avocado
beetroot
bok choy
broccoli
brussel sprouts
cabbage
carrot
cauliflower
celeriac
celery
chestnut
cumquat
custard apple
endive

fennel
garlic
ginger
grapefruit
hazelnut
horseradish
Jerusalem artichoke
kohlrabi
leek
lemon
lime
mandarin
okra
olive
onion

orange
parsnip
pear
potato
pumpkin
rhubarb
shallots
silverbeet
spinach
swede
sweet potato
tangelo
turnip
walnut
witlof

Late winter (August)

apple	fennel	parsnip
artichoke	garlic	pawpaw
avocado	ginger	pear
beetroot	grapefruit	pineapple
bok choy	horseradish	potato
broccoli	Jerusalem artichoke	pumpkin
brussel sprouts	kohlrabi	rhubarb
cabbage	leek	shallots
carrot	lemon	silverbeet
cauliflower	lime	spinach
celeriac	mandarin	swede
celery	okra	sweet potato
cumquat	olive	tangelo
custard apple	onion	turnip
endive	orange	witlof

Index of ailments

A

abdominal pain 114, 159, 160, 167, 175, 180, 181, 182

acne 16, 18, 34, 35, 50, 52, 149, 151, 166

alcoholism 12, 13, 39, 61, 125, 126, 146, 148, 153, 165, 166, 171, 182

allergies 35, 38, 182

anaemia 31, 38, 98, 120, 128, 130, 155, 157, 161, 164, 166, 167, 170, 179, 187

anorexia 63, 149, 156, 161

anxiety 3, 57, 120, 169

appetite issues 14, 23, 27, 56, 57, 62, 89, 91, 95, 113, 116, 117, 125, 128, 130, 152, 153, 155, 156, 157, 161, 164, 169, 173, 174, 183, 185

artery hardening 58, 62, 147, 150, 172, 182

arthritis 20, 29, 35, 60, 75, 89, 114, 117, 120, 125, 130, 138, 143, 144, 146, 150, 153, 155, 161, 162, 166, 182

asthma 16, 20, 85, 87, 88, 90, 114, 121, 130, 147, 160, 164, 166, 175, 187

B

back pain 98, 118, 120, 125, 130, 150, 167, 177, 186

bad breath 69, 173

bladder control 30, 177

bladder infection 59, 146, 155, 168

bleeding gum 168, 176

bloating 40, 56, 146

blurred vision 66, 129, 143, 150, 157, 162, 170, 179

boils 18, 161, 163

breathing 4, 31, 52, 60, 61, 63, 82, 83, 85, 86, 87, 89, 91, 116, 117, 142, 146, 147, 168, 170

bruising 30, 57, 148, 158, 172

burns 63, 146

burping 57, 91, 102, 125, 149, 165, 173, 175

C

chest congestion 184

chest pain 61, 63, 158, 180, 181

chilblains 154

cigarette smoking 147

circulation 6, 14, 15, 18, 19, 39, 54, 55, 56, 71, 77, 91, 95, 98, 102, 113, 114, 115, 116, 120, 125, 130, 151, 152, 155, 158, 161, 165, 168, 171, 172, 179, 180, 183, 186

conjunctivitis 33, 155, 160, 162, 163, 170, 174, 182, 187

constipation 16, 18, 19, 30, 31, 36, 52, 57, 82, 83, 84, 88, 89, 94, 102, 104, 105, 117, 146, 147, 148, 163, 165, 175, 176, 177, 179, 182, 183, 184, 189

cough 22, 40, 48, 59, 60, 82, 83, 84, 85, 86, 87, 88, 89, 102, 103, 105, 107, 146, 147, 158, 160, 162, 163, 164, 168, 170, 171, 172, 173, 174, 175, 176, 177, 178, 182, 185, 186, 187, 188, 189

D

deafness 116, 117, 167, 177

depression 29, 31, 35, 36, 54, 56, 62, 64, 91, 121, 136, 139, 140, 144, 152, 160, 171, 179, 180, 186, 188

diabetes 118, 128, 170, 184

diarrhoea 15, 16, 18, 19, 30, 31, 33, 38, 40, 56, 88, 90, 91, 92, 93, 94, 98, 101, 122, 125, 129, 146, 148, 149, 151, 153, 156, 157, 158, 160, 161, 162, 165, 166, 168, 169, 170, 171, 172, 175, 177, 179, 184, 186, 189

distension 33, 35, 57, 71, 89, 91, 146, 149, 157, 163, 170, 172, 174, 178, 182, 185, 187

dizziness 18, 28, 31, 36, 44, 54, 64, 79, 88, 98, 118, 143, 146, 152, 162, 168, 170, 176, 180, 181, 183, 185

Index of recipes